Managing the Classroom

Preparing Students for a Career-Ready Future

Eva Marie Foxwell

CR Teaching Inc.

Copyright 2017 by Eva Marie Foxwell

All rights reserved, including the right to reproduce this book or portion thereof in any form whatsoever. In accordance with U.S. law, the scanning, uploading and electronic sharing of any part of this book without the permission of the publisher constitutes unlawful piracy and theft of the author's intellectual property.

Thank you for your support of the author's rights.

Originally published in paperback and ebook by CR Teaching Inc.
May 2017

Published by CR Teaching Inc.

CRTeaching.com

Managing the Classroom/Eva Marie Foxwell. – 2nd ed. August 2018

ISBN: 978-0-9989291-1-8 (eBook)
ISBN: 978-0-9989291-0-1 (paperback)

Dedication

To my mother, Lillian V. Zanolini, who always believed in my teaching abilities and was the sunshine of my life.

To my cousin, Dennis L. Kormonick, who guided me toward the education field and was instrumental in all aspects of my life.

To my "WONDER WOMAN" sister, Anita Schwartz, who has been my true inspiration throughout my entire life.

Praise for Eva Foxwell's Methodology and Outcomes

"Your students were outstanding. You should be very proud. I'm cc'ing Amanda to schedule a visit. Thanks!"
- Delaware Governor Jack Markell

"Eva is an extraordinary teacher, a respected leader among her colleagues, and a kind and generous human being devoted to helping students succeed...I have watched Eva grow as an educator and witnessed how the work she has done with her students continues to evolve and challenges them to greater things. She consistently goes above and beyond, developing a highly successful Business program, earning a Superstar in Education Award and a lifelong influence on her students."

- Hugh Broomall, Ed.D. Deputy Superintendent

"Business Technology has given my daughter tools that she will utilize throughout her entire life. The material is presented in a 'real world' way. There are direct links made by class as to how this sort of organization and process will help them better succeed and achieve their goals."

- Parent

Table of Contents

Introduction	1
How This Book is Organized	5
Student Learning Outcomes	9
A Special Note on Communication Skills	10
Successful Students	11
A Note on Differentiated Instruction	14
Part I: Classroom Expectations	17
Best Practices	19
Refocusing the classroom	19
Respect and fairness	21
Good and Bad Bosses	32
Quality of Work	36
Classroom Motto	38
Requesting Assistance	40
Written Communication	41
Time Management	42
Classroom structure	43
Preventing boredom	43
Incomplete assignments	43
A Typical Morning in My Classroom	45

Putting Expectations into Practice	47
Part II: Classroom Procedures	**51**
Classroom Performance	52
Classroom Assessment	53
Classroom Transitioning	55
Classroom Procedures	57
Student Organization	58
Course Syllabus	60
Part III: Positions for Classroom Jobs	**63**
Selecting Positions	64
The Boss/ Business Manager/ Teacher	65
Assistant Manager Positions	69
Project Manager Positions	74
Quality Assurance Manager Positions	76
Marketing Manager Positions	77
Transition Manager Positions	80
Attendance Manager Positions	82
Scribe Manager Positions	84
Timekeeper Positions	85
Positions for Classroom Jobs Chart	87
Getting Started with Lesson Plans	88
Part IV: Enacting Your Lesson Plans	**93**

Example Day Ice Breaker — 93

    Students Entering the Classroom — 93
    Warm Up — 96
    Introduction — 97
    Communication Development — 98
    Student Independent Development — 100
    Providing Constructive Feedback — 101
    Closure — 102
    Students Departing the Classroom — 102

Example Day Setting Goals — 103

    Students Entering the Classroom — 103
    Introduction — 103
    Development — 104
    Student Independent Development — 108
    Closure — 108
    Students Departing the Classroom — 109

Example Day Learning Style Exercise — 109

    Students Entering the Classroom — 109
    Warm Up — 110
    Introduction — 110
    Class Development — 111
    Student Group Development — 115

Closure	119
Students Departing the Classroom	120
Example Day Learning Type Chart Exercise	**120**
Students Entering the Classroom	120
Warm Up	121
Introduction	121
Class Development	122
Student Independent Development	123
Student Group Development	124
Closure	126
Students Departing the Classroom	126
A Note About Lesson Plan Consistency	**127**
About the Author	**129**

Introduction

Most 7th through 12th grade schools have incorporated business-based curriculums; however, many instructors lack the business experience necessary to create realistic context for their lesson plans. This leaves students unprepared to establish a strong foundation for hands-on experience in the workforce. I believe that we can better prepare students for the technology demands and the fast-paced professional environment that they will experience in the workplace.

But what does "career-ready" *really* mean? After working in business and management for over 20 years, I've come to define a career-ready individual as a person who can make decisions, problem-solve, engage in critical thinking, analyze situations to overcome problems, and set goals.

Grounded in these basic skills, I have developed a business curriculum that can be adapted to any classroom and any age of student. This manual differs from other classroom management guides in one prominent way: I manage my classroom by directly tying it to the curriculum. My students walk into my classroom, which transforms itself from a standard computer lab into a bustling and productive business environment.

In this manual, I will show you how to lay the groundwork for your own classroom and provide you with examples to create as realistic of a career-ready environment for your students as possible.

I'm doing this because my primary goal in teaching is to make education a memorable and enjoyable experience for all students so that they can walk the path of success. If I had to condense my entire philosophy into a bulleted list that I would ask other teachers to internalize and employ in their classrooms, it would look something like this:

- **Hands-on learning keeps students interested**—The more the students are engaged with learning, the more they want to learn. Getting them excited about learning through hands-on activities ultimately helps them retain more information.

- **Connect with your students**—The best way to tell if your student is understanding the material and succeeding is to monitor them as well as engage with them. Understand that all students learn differently and need to be taught based on their specific learning styles. Analyze each student to know how they best learn and retain information.

- **Strategize, adapt, modify, change**—The business world demands that you be flexible. If something isn't working, you don't let it continue to fail. Instead, you develop a new plan and you fix it. In much the same way, if a student isn't succeeding or engaging with your material, you must develop and implement a new strategy. Sometimes it takes a few tries to find a tactic that works. (You'll see an example of a strategy I use to help struggling students in differentiated instruction.)

- **Tell stories**—In my class I tell stories, lots of stories. I talk about times I've failed, times I've succeeded, and times I felt nervous in addition to unprepared. I share my experiences with my students because they can learn from me just as your students can learn from you. Even if you don't have many real-life experiences to share, get creative so you can identify with the students. Whether the story was real matters little compared to whether the students learned something important from the story.

- **Provide real feedback**—Student are reviewing comments and I am encouraging constructive dialogue during class times. These are crucial feedback mechanisms from which you can help students identify areas of growth and weakness. Help students recognize their mistakes and work with them to identify strategies to improve. Also, no student is perfect; you aren't doing any favors to the students who are already succeeding if you don't push them to be even better.

- **Tell the students you care**—Sometimes students have this idea that teachers don't care about their education. Prove them wrong! Remind them of it all the time. You may be surprised at what a difference this can make. Simply add statements such as, "You know I really care about your future so I am teaching you skills that will make you stand out as a performer. I know what you need to succeed and that's exactly what I am trying to do. Please know I have your best interest in mind and I want you to shine." When you share these sentiments in your conversations with students, you begin to develop a nurturing relationship with them. When they think you care, they care, too.

- **Have fun**—I never want my class to be boring. All of my lessons include hands-on activities and "live" scenarios to actively engage students with the curriculum and with each other. Through these activities, my students gain an in-depth understanding of what it's like to work in a fast-paced environment with a focus on time management, leadership, and organization. It's incredible to discover the students' level of performance when they understand the material, care about the results of their work, and have fun in class.

- **Continue learning**—It is so crucial to stay abreast of all the changes in your field by taking education classes. By pursuing your education, not only will you be more knowledgeable, you will also provide your students with the best learning experience.

Throughout my time working as a business teacher, I have spoken to students outside of my school district and asked them what they were learning in business or technology. After hearing about their experiences, I have come to realize business skills are not being taught effectively enough in the classroom. I knew I needed to share the experiences in my classroom with other educators.

I have an opportunity to help other business teachers, elementary school teachers, middle school teachers, high school teachers, and other educators understand life in the business world. I also want to give them access to all of my materials. That is why I was inspired to create a multi-volume series that I will revise to keep up with new trends in business. I feel that writing various manuals to target specific lesson groups will reach a larger audience; more teachers will be able to utilize the curriculum and achieve success for themselves and their students.

How This Book is Organized

This manual lays the groundwork for developing a successful and practical course for the development of career-ready students. This classroom management strategy can be adapted into any environment with students of any age. While I provide specific examples (and more lesson plans in accompanying editions as well as online), you should tailor your class to their needs and available resources. The goal is to provide you with classroom management techniques and blended learning activities to simulate 'real world' experiences that improves student learning and retention to ultimately provide the necessary skills in order for students to excel in any occupation.

Callouts Used in This Book

Throughout this manual you will see four roles used as "callouts" to indicate specific types of information that will give you a quick reference to the topics listed below.

Boss	This callout indicates an example of something I would say to my students as their boss. These examples are designed to give you a look into how I speak with my students in the classroom and how I explain certain business topics. You should always tailor your own speech to your comfort level and to the needs of your students.
Manager	This callout is when the students are demonstrating their role as the manager for their specific job positions.

Student/ Employees	This callout describes the responsibility of the students within the classroom.
Tips	This callout is specific information that I want to draw your attention to more closely. These tips will provide more in-depth information or a practical application of the subject being covered in that section.

Terminology you'll see throughout this book

Throughout this text I will consistently use certain "buzzwords" that have a specific meaning in my classroom. In an effort to help you understand them and their implications, I've created a list of the most common buzzwords I use and their meanings.

Additionally, I have also included some industry words and their exact definitions because they might be slightly different than your understanding of the word.

Tip: I also make sure that my students understand these terms because I often use them when I want them to complete a task.

1. ***Transitioning*** is a time when the students have to effectively move from one place to another without wasting time. In the business world, it is important to be respectful of customers; students must be very quiet as to not interrupt "customers" who are on the telephone line with our representatives.

2. ***Directives*** are instructions dictated by management aimed at causing effective production to occur. Students (i.e. employees) must stop whatever they are doing and listen attentively to their manager to demonstrate respect and an eagerness to assist.

3. ***Announcements*** are when managers provide specific information about an activity that affects all or most of the people working in the classroom. Care should be taken that announcements are not to be made needlessly so they do not continuously interrupt work.

4. ***Business soft skills*** are skills associated with a person's emotional intelligence. It consists of a cluster of personality traits, language, communication, approachability, personal habits, and optimism that represents relationships with other people.

5. ***Producing at a high level*** means students will consistently be working and focusing on the tasks and projects assigned. It means that students are effectively completing assignments within strict time constraints.

6. ***Manager vs boss vs teacher*** is the person who has the most seniority or authority and is responsible for all final decisions made for the team. While these roles are usually fulfilled by the same person, each role has slightly different goals, objectives, and responsibilities.

7. A ***syllabus*** explains grading, expectations, and assignments for the students. This document should be distributed and explained to students on the first day of class.

8. ***Student job responsibilities*** are the tasks that students have as part of their job assigned to them for the classroom. These are reviewed in depth in Part III.

9. ***Organizational binders*** are the binders that I have my students bring to every class where they place their work so they stay organized. I periodically check the layout of these binders to enforce good organizational habits.

10. ***Time is money*** is a phrase I use frequently to remind students that when time is wasted, it costs money. The goal is to make students aware that they are "being paid" to complete assignments and that they must work productively.

11. ***Business world*** is used to generally describes and includes the culture and environment of commercial operations or companies.

Student Learning Outcomes

In a business environment, there are hard skills and soft skills—in my classroom, I teach both. In this particular manual, I emphasize the soft skills because often times that is what is lacking most in the classroom. The soft skills in focus throughout this manual are

- <u>Communication</u> and how it plays a huge role in performing your everyday job responsibilities.

- <u>Time Management</u> and its part in managing your task list, meetings, and assignments effectively throughout the day in order to meet deadlines.

- <u>Respect and Fairness</u> and how it is necessary for the morale of the team.

- <u>Teamwork</u> and working together to accomplish the goals as well as objectives of the company.

- <u>Leadership</u> and taking the initiative to assist others, lead others, and set a good example for people to follow.

- <u>Persistence</u> and the benefits of ensuring the assignments get completed no matter how long it will take.

- <u>Organization</u> and the ability to be able to find and access information quickly.

Many of these skills will be mentioned several times throughout the text and it is important to note the different contexts in which they are used.

A Special Note on Communication Skills

I have found that in recent years face-to-face communication skills have diminished even in younger students due to electronic devices. They often don't know how to converse appropriately during basic conversations. It is my goal to leave them with a conversational skill set that will ingratiate them with their future employers and have an overall positive impact for the rest of their lives.

I teach my students the following skills to become better conversationalists.

- Greetings
- Appropriate eye contact
- Facial expressions and other nonverbal indicators of active listening
- Appropriate verbal responses
- Deferring judgement and determining the appropriate time to ask questions
- Closing statements

When developing your course and throughout the school year, pay attention to the needs of your students. If your students come into your classroom able to communicate well (or if they learn that skill quickly), adjust your plans to focus on their weak spots. Perhaps time management will plague your students, maybe it's teamwork, or something else entirely. Remember, you must model business world behaviors and that means being able to adjust, improve, and adapt!

Successful Students

Success is an important topic that I continually discuss with my students. One of the best measures of success in the classroom is whether your students are meeting the student learning outcomes that you've established. You will know when your students have achieved the student learning outcomes when they

- Understand all classroom expectations and communicate effectively by demonstrating strong emotional intelligence.
- Demonstrate strong time management by completing assignments within the time allotted.
- Emulate respect and fairness to their boss, their coworkers, and others.
- Initiate teamwork to accomplish more assignments.
- Act according to directives administered by the boss and act as a leader to their peers.
- Persist through difficult assignments.
- Exhibit organizational skills by jotting down notes and maintaining an organized class binder.

I have found in my many years in business and teaching that achieving personal success is similar to walking on a path. Each step gets you closer to or further from your goals. Much like a path in the woods, the road to success is not always straight and well defined. I think it is crucial for my students to understand this concept so I take time to explain this to my students. I do this through wisdom excerpts like the one below.

Boss: "Walking the path of success is an important long-term goal. Life is like walking on a path. You may venture off the path and make mistakes, but overall as long as you learn from those mistakes, you will be able to get right back on the path and continue achieving success. I want to emphasize that making mistakes is acceptable and makes you stronger individuals. There isn't a single successful person that achieved success without making any mistakes. If anything, they made many mistakes and ultimately it made them stand out and become better at what they did."

How students feel about class is important. If your students are bored, intimidated, or feeling negatively about your class, they will not learn successfully; they will not retain as much information. It can be difficult to mitigate how students feel about your class while also providing a challenging curriculum.

I find that the primary reason my students like the classroom environment I create is because it gives them responsibility and makes them feel "grown up". It is important to recognize why your students enjoy (or do not enjoy) your class. I have found that in my classroom the more responsibility I give them, the happier they are overall simply because they have a purpose. Specifically, students have told me that they like

- Having specific jobs that they are responsible for every day.
- Having jobs with expectations and responsibilities.
- Participating as leaders in team meetings.
- Voicing their opinions to make suggestions and/or improvements to the performance of class or to a specific project.

- Having the freedom to assist other students at any time during class in order to stay on task as a team.
- Making important decisions for the increased production of the team.
- Understanding the importance of organization and how it plays an integral role in their performance.

Take note about what motivates your students to respond and what gets them excited. Again, manipulate the lessons and practices in this manual to fit your students and your classroom. The more you modify your lesson plan, the better it will become in the long run.

When you implement the methods and practices that I have laid out for you in this text, your students will learn much more than the standard curriculum.

- They will be more aware of time and how they are spending it.
- They will understand the importance of customers and their relationship to job stability.
- They will learn to complete assignments for their boss that are neat and organized.
- They will understand how to take pride in their work.
- They will learn to identify problems and find reasonable solutions.
- They will understand how to be patient and practice self-control.
- They will understand how their overall behavior relates to the boss' perception of them.

- They will understand the need to demonstrate a positive attitude.
- They will gain confidence in their abilities.
- They will understand the importance of being responsible.
- They will understand how to emulate respect.
- They will learn to work together as a team.

You might even find: quiet students become outgoing; troubled students find a purpose to excel; followers become leaders; negativity becomes positivity; complaining becomes proactively finding solutions; questions become more purposeful; and students become more self-reliant.

A Note on Differentiated Instruction

There are many cases where differential instruction is needed, and in my classes I assign mentors to the students who are struggling. There are several reasons that this can be a successful arrangement, but it is important to incorporate this situation into the classroom appropriately.

After explaining the importance of teamwork to my students, they know that they can assist one another as needed. As the manager I encourage students to converse with others if someone needs assistance. This is where I explain about the principle of "I can, you can, we can" to help them understand that it's not always just about them individually, it's also about working together as a team.

Boss: "Working together as a team is crucial in effectively achieving goals and assignments for the business. You may not necessarily like everyone in your group, but you must focus on the end result of the assignment that your boss is asking you to complete and simply get it done. There is no time to complain since there are always time limits associated with production."

Given the nature of the classroom, you will need to monitor these interactions very carefully and ensure that the mentor is still able to complete his or her own work on time. I have had great success with this method and I often see increased production from both students.

I have found that by using peers to bridge a learning gap, confidence increases with the struggling student and the mentor feels important. I am also constantly assisting students in need of additional help throughout the lesson.

I explain to my students that everyone learns differently and it is my job to find the most effective ways to make learning successful for each student. It is very helpful for the students to take the time to understand their own learning style, and I provide an example of those lessons plans and activities in this manual. I explain to them that if they understand their learning style, they can increase their productivity (thus decreasing the amount of time and effort that it takes to understand a concept or complete an assignment).

To help them determine their learning styles, I have each student take a computer assessment to understand if they are a visual, audio, or tactile learner. I also use the information about their learning styles to substantiate my lesson plans. I know it is more difficult and time consuming to teach that way and time is often on the short side, but I find that putting in the effort to tailor my lessons makes my students more successful and helps them enjoy learning. In my classroom, I find that there is consistently a high percentage of tactile learners so my overall hands-on learning approach is geared towards them. I always ensure that I accommodate the other types of learners by using visual aids and oral communication as well. The students become more confident and want to produce at a higher level because they are being taught in the most effective way.

Part I: Classroom Expectations

Expectations are crucial to the success of a classroom and the effectiveness of a curriculum. Below, I share my list of expectations that I have for my classroom and my students, posted just like the workplace must have Labor Laws posted in their employee areas. When creating your own list, make sure that it embodies your classroom environment and your teaching style and personality.

Here are my classroom expectations.

- Respect peers and management
- Demonstrate fairness
- Complete daily classroom warm ups
- Understand how the classroom motto impacts performance
- Write in cursive
- Apply effective time management skills
- Complete assignments after being absent
- Take pride in all work assignments
- Assist other students
- Understand the importance of quality and quantity
- Organize a portfolio binder
- Become a leader
- Communicate effectively with peers and adults
- Accept constructive criticism

- Produce the highest quality work within the given time
- Understand the business environment
- Understand the impact of a person's actions in the business world
- Gain the respect of others
- Ask questions effectively
- Speak effectively in front of an audience
- Understand the importance of team meetings
- Work independently and with groups

In the following sections I address certain aspects of my classroom expectations, too, so that you understand how I apply them and how you might apply them in your classroom.

Once the students understand my expectations, the classroom takes on a positive atmosphere that ultimately makes the students receptive to and prepared for a more intensive workload. The students often don't even realize all the work they are completing because they are having fun and they understand what I expect from them.

If you find that you are not consistently applying your classroom expectations (nearly) every day, then it might be time to review your list and either find ways to apply the expectation daily or determine if the expectation is worthwhile.

Best Practices

When my students come into class each day, they have a specific routine that they follow to set the tone for each lesson, which sets the stage for meeting classroom expectations. Every student is expected to complete certain classroom duties (as part of an assigned role or as a part of a devoted time during class), which will be described in more detail in the section on enacting the lesson plan.

Just like in the business world, where you are expected to adhere to the job expectations, policies, and procedures of your employer, in my classroom the students are expected to act like employees. By following a routine they gain an understanding of my overall expectations for their behavior in addition to productivity starting from the minute they walk into the classroom.

Tip: Remember that your classroom expectations should be reinforced every day because they are crucial for the success of the student's individual performance as well as the success of the team. Creating a structured warm up exercise or start-of-class routine can help your students start the day off right and get them in the learning mindset.

Refocusing the classroom

Sometimes I find it necessary to remind all of my students that what they are learning is important and that completing their work to a high-standard is crucial to their overall performance. When I remind my students of this, I also want them to understand my stake in their education because they should know that I care about what happens in my classroom.

Tip: Because I run my classroom like a business, I try to draw parallels wherever I can between the expectations of the classroom and the expectations of an employer. Classroom expectations can be a great way to do this.

Here's something I might say to express the importance of their tasks:

Boss: "My promise to you is to strive to make all the learning activities and lessons in this class consistent with the district's grade level standards (then related it to business). Every activity is purposeful and engaging. Each lesson should be another step toward meeting and exceeding the school district's standards (how to work in a business environment). I want all of you to know that I have a clear purpose in your education; I want you to surpass the goals and expectations that are requested from you. I will teach you how to accomplish this through the valuable lessons in this class."

By formally recognizing and identifying your role to your students, you can encourage a professional relationship with them. It makes it clear that while you have expectations for them, you also have expectations for yourself. Establishing this relationship will increase the likelihood that the students will accept and respect your role and fulfill their own roles as well.

Respect and fairness

When I meet students for the first time, I explain the importance of how respect and fairness are essential when communicating and working with others. Mutual respect is necessary for positive interactions to take place, and positive interactions increase performance.

Boss: "I remember working in the business world with a Senior Executive Vice President and I remembered her being fair with all the employees on our team. It created a great team environment so I want you to know I will always be fair in every aspect of this class. My boss basically treated everyone equally and never exhibited any favoritism, thus creating a positive and happy environment. Please know that as your teacher I will always be fair with you so I do not have favorites because you are all my favorites."

A great way to begin is to get to know all of your students by showing an interest in their education, perhaps by learning about their current family and living situation. Doing this can provide you with an opportunity to assess the student's current life and can help you identify the way in which each student learns as well as identify some of their personal struggles.

Tip: Here are some specific ways to connect with your students.

- Ask them about their weekend.
- Ask them what activities they are involved in outside of class.
- Observe their behavior at lunch to determine the type of student interactions that take place.

- If you notice they aren't interactive with many children, ask if the student wants to eat lunch in your room so they feel more comfortable without the entire class. I usually tell them that I need their assistance with a task and it opens up the opportunity for them to talk while I listen. Sometimes they just need someone to listen, not give instructions.
- Tell them stories about your life so they know it's ok to talk about theirs.
- Stop and talk to them in the hallway to ask them how their day is going.
- Tell them you need their help so they feel a sense of importance and a sense of being needed.
- Provide positive compliments and observe their response.
- Recognize a difference in their behavior and have a private discussion to ensure everything is ok.
- Buy them lunch and just talk.

By conversing with my students in this way, I ensure that they feel comfortable talking with me and asking for support or guidance when needed. This provides comfort for the students to have an open door for learning and other experiences in life.

In student and teacher interactions, a.k.a. fostering a respectful relationship, I believe that the success of my curriculum hinges on a healthy and respectful relationship between teacher and student. My curriculum and teaching style sometimes demands that I openly address un-business-like behavior in class.

Because I have to mimic how a boss would treat their adult subordinate, the interaction between my student and myself can sometimes seem very assertive. If you don't appear to respect your students or if you don't have a good relationship with them, these interactions won't be successful.

Boss: I always tell my students, "that was the boss talking and I want you to know that is the way your manager will communicate it in the business world, so be respectful and listen to your boss."

Something that surprises me most when I ask students outside of my school district about their relationship with their teachers they often tell me that their teachers don't acknowledge them when they come into class—no "hello" or "good morning" or "how are you doing today?" They are told just to get to work on their assignments. You wouldn't walk into your office without somehow verbally acknowledging your boss and other coworkers, so why do that to your students? It is very important to make your students feel like you are aware and pleased by their presence in class. You have to model the behavior that you want them to exhibit.

Another crucial factor in fostering a respectful relationship is to verbally remind your students that you care about them. There are a number of ways that you can show them you care, but all "tough love" with no positive reinforcement will make them feel defeated or uninterested in the class. I always say to my students "you know how much I care about you, and your future right?" and they always respond with a resounding yes. They can accept my constructive criticism more readily when they know that it comes from a place of caring and respect.

I've developed a list of ways that you can foster positive relationships with your students in a business-like manner. Employ these in your classroom. Remind yourself of them daily. Individually these actions may seem small, but they build the foundation for a successful curriculum.

Use this checklist to mark which of these tactics you have tried with your students. Write yourself notes about which ones worked for you and which ones didn't. Keeping track of the things you are saying to your students can help you recognize areas for your own improvement. I have grouped these interactions into three categories based on where they work best. Group relationship tactics are best deployed in the classroom and directed to the whole class. Individual relationship tactics are best for determining who is struggling and then with whom you should use the individual crisis relationship tactics.

Class Relationship Development Tactics Checklist

1. Tell the class how much you like them and will always wish the best for them.

2. Let the class know you genuinely care about their future and all the experiences that are involved with being in school.

3. Tell the class how proud you are that you are their teacher.

4. Tell the class you feel honored to teach them.

5. Verbalize to the class how well they are performing.

6. Tell the class they are the best students EVER!

7. Tell the class, "Do you know how much I care about your future? A lot. I want the best for you so I promise you I will provide the best educational experience."

8. Ask the class how they are doing. It shows you care about them and make them feel better about performing in class.

9. Have daily team meetings with the class to ensure effective communication takes place.

10. Tell the class how far they will go in life because of their strong performance.

11. Verbalize to the class that you believe in them.

12. Tell the class how impressed that they work together as a team.

13. Express to your students how much you enjoy your job.

Individual Relationship Development Tactics Checklist

1. Smile.

2. Stand by the door when the students arrive and depart.

3. Greet them by saying, "Happy Monday, Happy Tuesday, Happy Wednesday, Happy Thursday, Happy Friday."

4. Say "hello" to your students as they walk into your classroom every day.

5. Be pleasant.

6. Consistently touching base with your students on their performance as you are walking around the room is a must.

7. Just being genuine, yet assertive, is an advantage with students.

8. Actively listen to the students at all times while looking them in the eyes.

9. Exhibited a good mood so they are in a good mood.

10. Try and think about the ways you would want to learn and adding fun into the mixture.

11. Make comments to the students on a personal level, your haircut looks great, you dressed so nice, you carry yourself so professionally, you are respectful, I'm impressed with your performance, you've got so much potential.

12. Tell a lot of stories about work and life that inspire the students and grabs their attention.

13. Being happy makes the classroom always have a positive feel to it.
14. Be reliable for students when they need you.
15. Show how you work hard to create every lesson so they, too, will work hard. Show all your lesson plans and explain that you took the time to create all of them because they deserve it and you want them to learn.
16. Say things like you are the best, you are awesome, wow, great job, fantastic, impressive, great work, excellent, fantastic, amazing, proud of you, incredible.
17. Make the students feel important by asking them to assist you or obtain their opinion.
18. Make sure the students know all the decisions you make as a teacher are for a really good reason and for their future.
19. Provide a sufficient amount of time to complete their classwork.
20. Ask the students other than your class about personal activities happening in their lives, sports, family, etc.
21. Thank students for completing assignments and tasks because it shows the importance in the business world how a manager is thankful for the work that is getting accomplished.
22. Encourage students to work hard to obtain success.

Individual Crisis Tactics Checklist

1. Try to provide a mindset for students to work harder. Things like, "How would your manager react in a real business situation." There are two quotes without punctuation. Is that correct? "I'm going to a meeting so do have the paperwork that we discussed from 2 weeks ago?"
2. Be positive no matter what difficult circumstances are going on in my own personal life. I focus on doing what is right for the students and their education. Trust me there are hard days, but they deserve to have a great day even if yours is not so great.
3. Explain how nothing in life is perfect, but no matter what you do it can always be improved.
4. Focus on being positive when you see students that are struggling. Build their confidence rather than break it down.
5. Tell the students that it's ok to make mistakes as long as they learn from them.

Managers view people by their body language, including how they sit, their facial expressions, and general attitude towards receiving directives. Employees who regularly demonstrate respectful body language and behavior will likely be candidates for promotion over those who don't.

When you (as the teacher and their boss) speak, all students should turn around and look directly at you to show you that they are actively listening. You should reinforce positive student behavior and continually apply the classroom expectations.

I have found that tough love is best administered by the Boss. It is your job to convince the students that not completing an assignment can impact their job in a negative way. They always need to complete the work that is assigned to them because there is a consequence for not completing work in the business world. Explain that students could possibly be placed on corrective action, on a performance plan, demoted, or simply fired.

On the other hand, you should ensure that you recognize the positives of completing work as well. Make sure you explain that if employees are supportive, hard workers and reliable to their manager, then the manager will be fair when it comes to promotions and pay raises.

Respectful Behavior

To reinforce and encourage positive student behavior in the business context, I use phrases like these below to tie the classroom expectations to the expectations of an employer.

- "Good try, let's see how we can work on it together."
- "Your performance is great. I'm proud to be your manager."
- "I like the way you are assisting your co-worker."
- "You are all working together as a team, which is crucial for meeting our company goals."
- "Look to your co-workers on both sides of you and tell them 'great job'."
- "I couldn't have asked for better employees to work with me."

- "Thank you for working so hard. The work you've done is crucial for this large project and you are to be commended."
- "All of you are excellent employees and I am ecstatic about your performance."
- "Time is money so let's get this assignment completed for the administrative boss."
- "The potential you have is unbelievable so your effort is appreciated."
- "WOW, you are a great employee."
- "I appreciate the way you are working to achieve our monthly goals."
- "It's comforting to know I can step away to go to a meeting and come back to great production."
- "It's amazing how great you work together as a team."
- "Your performance surpasses the business expectations."
- "You all amaze me based on your attitude and positive interactions."
- "I'm so happy you work for me."

Tip: The way in which you run your classroom should be consistent. Because I run my classroom like a business, I make sure that I carry that idea into the daily interactions with my students. If one day you are acting like the classroom is a business but the next you are not, you run the risk of confusing the students and weakening the outcomes of your efforts. Consistency is the key.

Disrespectful Behavior

When a student is displaying disrespectful behavior, it is important to address the situation immediately. It is important to frame your responses in the right context--should you address this conflict in the context of the "boss" or in the context of the "teacher"?

When addressing issues as a teacher, try to also mention the way a boss would treat this issue. This can help students recognize the severity of their actions and make them more cognizant of their present behavior.

Conversely, when addressing disrespectful behavior as the boss, you should clearly identify how "liking" your boss is different than "respecting" your boss. For example, here is something I might say to a student in private who is having difficulties with respect:

Boss: "It's not so much about liking me as a boss, but it is important to respect me. I want you to know your behavior is unacceptable and do you understand the negative effect that would result in if you worked in the business world? You could get demoted, be placed on a performance plan, and/or get fired. You need to think before you act and decide what is important as far as your job and career. If you end up getting fired because of your low performance or misbehavior, you would have to go home to your family and tell them you were fired when they depend on your income. You need to understand your behavior affects other people as well. I want you to live a successful life so please know I care and want what is best for you. Please tell me that you understand the impact of your actions."

I want to note here that there has never been an incident where the student rebelled or said that they did not understand my conversation. Putting behavior into context outside the classroom can correct some issues that typical classroom admonishment could not. I also verbalize that they have a job to perform and not meeting the expectations will result in disciplinary actions.

Tip: I've actually created termination and performance plan example letters and administered them to students to make them understand the severity to their actions when the situation calls for this business-like example. I make them sign it and explain it will be placed in their file for the remainder of their time with the company (this class). Also, I note that it may hinder the ability to get a promotion because other bosses review files before making their decisions to hire people. I explain that a copy of their letter goes to Human Resources, who are responsible for employee relations, payroll, benefits, training, recruiting, screening, interviewing, and placing workers within the company. After reading the letters, the student truly grasps the concept and the misbehavior diminishes.

Good and Bad Bosses

Respect from your students is crucial, but it is also a two-way street. Without mutual respect, the team's and business' performance doesn't usually go as expected. I find that it is important to discuss with my students the differences between good and bad managers. Just as there are good and bad employees, there are good and bad managers. Make it clear that the expectations of the classroom also apply to you as a boss and a teacher.

Referring back to an earlier example of discussing equality with my students, I use the example of one on my managers who never had favorites and treated all employees equally, which made our team successful. The atmosphere that her fairness created enabled the team to excel and work at high levels. Based on my experiences I've created a list of qualities that you can find in a good manager. A good manager/boss:

- Communicates clearly and always makes sure the employees are kept up to date.
- Participative, present, and available for their employees.
- Recognizes employees for their achievements and performance.
- Sets a good example, such as consistency.
- Demonstrates active listening skills.
- Demonstrates organization.
- Provides constructive feedback.
- Is specific in his or her requests.
- Is patient.
- Is honest.
- Is genuine.
- Creates a positive environment.
- Demonstrates concern for the wellbeing and success of the team.
- Practices being fair.
- Encourages creativity as well as "outside-the-box" thinking.
- Admits to and recognizes errors.
- Acknowledges the skills of team members.

- Is open to new ideas.
- Is available for questions, support, and other interactions.
- Keeps abreast of the business changes.
- Exhibits strong emotional and intellectual intelligence.
- Demonstrates strong people skills.
- Truly cares about employee opinions and wellbeing of the team.
- Has an interest in his or her employee's future.

Tip: Use a personal story (or create one) to illustrate important points. Explain how there was one manager in your previous experience that was the most impressive and impactful because a particular trait they possessed.

I have experienced many different management styles working in the business world. Here's a list of things in a bad manager/boss, and likely everyone can make these stories more relatable with a boss you or a friend has had during employment:

- **Always Right.** They always point out how everyone else is wrong and they are right.
- **Poor Communicator.** Not providing clear directives leads to unfinished work and incorrect work.
- **Not A Good Listener.** They interrupt constantly, and don't really care about your suggestions or opinions.
- **Narcissist.** They think about themselves, Me Me Me, rather than the team

- **Screamer.** This is damaging mentally and does not assist students to performing better
- **Bully.** Bullies manage through fear and intimidation.
- **Unapologetic.** They never want to apologize for their mistakes.
- **Suck Up.** Spending little time with the people they manage and worrying about how they can look good in their boss's eyes.
- **Never Praise or Encourage.** They criticize and rarely ever praise their employees.
- **Not Honest.** Will say anything to appease people.
- **Avoids Challenging Issues.** They avoid having to face the confrontation that needs to be addressed.
- **Degrades**. Talks down to people and belittles them.
- **Never Praises**. Does not apply positive remarks.
- **Indecisive.** Not being confident in their position or ability to make the best decisions.
- **Micromanager.** Always looking over your shoulder while working.
- **Manipulative.** Trying to scheme and manipulate others in a negative way.
- **Vindictive.** If the boss feels threatened by an employee's comment or opinion, the boss may get back at them because he or she is insecure.
- **Demanding.** They insist on always telling you what to do rather than get your opinion.

- **Laissez Faire.** They don't ever seem to be there to support or step in to defend their employees.
- **Autocratic.** Center the business on themselves rather than their employees.
- **Delegates too much.** Rather than do their job, they delegate aspects of their position that others are not qualified to do.
- **No Expectations.** Not setting clear expectations for the employees.
- **Unmotivated.** The boss does not work as hard as the employees.
- **Standoffish.** Seems to not have a connection with the employees and feels uncomfortable communicating or even participating in a conversation.

Quality of Work

Quality plays an integral role in performance. I constantly talk to the students about how quality and quantity make a huge difference in production.

Quality of work is important because in the business world, mistakes or a poor quality product can cost a company millions of dollars. However, the quantity of work completed is also important. If a company produces very little work, even if it is high-quality it will not likely result in growth.

Ultimately, there should be a balance between the two. It is your job to make sure you strike the right balance for your classroom. You know that there are certain learning objectives you must meet so you cannot move too slowly and focus solely on quality, but it also does your students no good to ignore quality altogether.

So how do you do both? Why, it's by applying classroom expectations consistently! As I've mentioned, the consistent application of classroom expectations helps the students produce extra work more efficiently. Since your students will be able to complete work more quickly, it will give you time to focus on the quality of work.

Here is a scenario I use to demonstrate the importance of work quality to my students:

Boss: "Just as the president plays a large role in our nation's future, I play a role in determining your educational future. So make sure that you take pride in all of your work since I will be reviewing it for accuracy. When you hand me an assignment, you should know you worked hard to make it the best it could be. As your boss, it will make a negative impression on me if your work is full of errors just as it will make an impression on me if I see it has been done well. Make sure you are making the right impression because these assignments are crucial for completing our company's goals and objectives."

In my classroom, students will accomplish assignments that require a tremendous amount of focus on the quality of work.

- Creating marketing flyers
- Demonstrating interactive Smart Board tasks
- Inserting Microsoft Office tables and charts into documents
- Participating in individual and group assignments
- Understanding Word document formatting

- Organizing a portfolio binder for organization
- Creating PowerPoint presentations with transitions and animations
- Demonstrating business communications role plays and scenarios
- Participating in oral presentations
- Increasing keyboarding skills through various software programs
- Performing daily warm ups
- Participating in team projects
- Participating in team meetings
- Participating as managers for the classroom

    I consistently remind my students in my comments and feedback that by practicing and improving their quality of work, they are learning a necessary skill for the business world.

Classroom Motto

    All businesses have a motto—it's what senior leadership reviews when determining the course of the company. It is what employees seek for inspiration and direction.

    Since my classroom (and soon yours) operates like a business, it makes sense to have some kind of motto. The motto for my classroom is **WE CAN DO IT!** My students understand that they can accomplish any task for any assignment if they set their minds to it. I chose the "we can do it" motto because students need to understand that if they think positively, it will encourage success.

Choose a motto that reflects one of the important tenets of your classroom and have the students verbally state the motto every time you ask. This enforces the importance of the motto and it should be taken very seriously.

Boss: "WHAT IS OUR MOTTO?"

Students/Employees: "WE CAN DO IT!"

Tip: It takes practice, but occasionally ask the question when they are really busy to see if they are listening, are able to multi-task, and respond quickly even though they are engrossed in their work. Try to make sure they are saying it with enthusiasm rather than a low monotone voice. If their response is in monotone voices, then make them say it again in an upbeat tone. Explain that they are saying this in front of their boss and they should want their boss to know they are happy to be there. Remind them if it's a monotone voice, your boss may make a perception that you might not be happy or you really just don't want to work for the company.

Boss: "REMEMBER… I'm your boss and I pay you, administer your performance appraisal for possible raises, and promote you, so you should always show me that you are positive about your work experience here at the company. Your interactions with me should be respectful and positive at all times."

Using a motto can increase the sense of camaraderie between students as well as remind them of the particular belief that your motto represents.

Requesting Assistance

At work in the business world, sometimes you will find yourself in need of assistance from your manager, but they may not be able to immediately help you. Oftentimes, you will need to find something to occupy yourself by continuing to work while you wait for your manager to have a moment to assist you. This directly relates to classroom experiences.

Explain to the students that they must raise their hand if they have a question and you will assist them as soon as possible. This forces the students to be patient and learn to jot down questions until you are able to assist them. They must understand there is only one teacher, so instruct them to be patient and communicate you will assist them as soon as possible. I always circulate the room and will never be sitting at my desk unless I have to check their organizational binders.

Boss: "Every minute counts in the business and classroom environment, so you will sometimes find yourself in need of assistance. However, you can't expect someone to drop all of his or her work that instant to help you. Jot down your questions and/or ask your peers to assist, if they can, until I am able to help you."

Getting students to practice this behavior helps them figure out how to manage their time when they are stalled on a particular task. They quickly learn to become more resourceful and think critically to figure out how to find the answers to their own questions. It's amazing how the students learn this skill throughout the semester and they become extremely resourceful, develop a strong desire to complete tasks by problem solving.

Written Communication

I require my students to submit their assignments in cursive writing. I have found that the students do not like this because many schools are not teaching cursive writing in their curriculum anymore and they do not necessarily see the benefit in learning. Nevertheless, I think it is an important skill to have, partially because it's faster to take notes in cursive, but also because there are scenarios where they may need to be able to read and write in cursive in the business environment (if you've ever had a boss who wrote in illegible writing on a memo, you know exactly how this feels).

For instance, what will they do if a customer sends them a note in cursive writing or if their boss leaves notations on their work in script? I ask my students to consider how they would go to their boss and tell him or her that they cannot read it. It is also a skill that is still necessary when signing a check, driver's license, buying a home, and even getting married. People still use cursive in the business world and it is important for students to be competent in this skill. In addition, there is a portion on the SATs where students have the option to print or write in cursive; writing in cursive is faster and will be advantageous time wise during the test.

I provide the students with a copy of the alphabet in cursive so they can keep it in their binder and reference it during class. Most of the students practice at home or in homeroom so they can develop their skills faster.

By the end of the semester, it's amazing how well they write and they, too, are surprised by their efforts. It's great to see that they are aware of their increased performance as well. I find students that originally printed in my previous classes are now writing in cursive consistently.

There are instances where I will allow them to print, but I tell them I have to give the authorization to make the change. The students then understand they have rules in the business world and must be aware that they have to be given permission before changing a process.

Time Management

It is important to take into account that all classes are different and you may extend the lesson based on the total classes' performance. If there are students that complete the assignment before others, they should always have a secondary activity that they can go to that will keep them learning and busy while they wait.

In my classroom, my students are required to go to any software program that lets them practice their keyboarding skills. Not only does this give the students the opportunity to focus on increasing their keyboarding skills, it also keeps the students learning at all times. It is very rare that any student will ever not have any work in my class. I feel every minute is valuable and that it is my job to ensure they are engaged 100% of the time, engrossed in learning.

There are other factors to time-management in the classroom, too.

Classroom structure

My classroom is structured into distinct time-frames so students are consistently working and completing the tasks and assignments asked by their "boss". I have segmented particular parts of the class for predictable assignments so that the students know what is expected of them within a particular time frame. Adding a time limit to tasks and assignments makes the students aware of utilizing their time management skills wisely.

Preventing boredom

Adding an associated time to every assignment allows the students to learn how to pace themselves and they understand there is never a moment where they have nothing to do. I feel my class provides a lot of interaction and incorporates time limits to diminish boredom or behavior issues. The key to limiting discipline problems is to ensure students are always engaged and completing their assignments so they do not have time to dawdle.

Incomplete assignments

Incomplete assignments from students are less frequent because I stress the importance of time throughout the class. As one of the job responsibilities (see Part III), there is a Timekeeper whose job is to mention the specific time throughout the class so the students can pace themselves for the assignment on which they are working. Emphasizing that completing the work their manager asks of them will result in a good performance appraisal and possibly a monetary raise.

I explain that it is unacceptable in the business environment to not complete work based on the deadline that their manager gives them. They may possibly be placed on corrective action or even fired depending upon the importance of the task and the lateness of the task. Emphasizing that there are consequences if they don't complete a task provides an incentive to work hard and complete work.

Boss: "There are a lot of assignments throughout each class that need to be completed, so you need to use your time wisely. If an assignment does not get completed in class, then all of you know it is to be completed as homework. I ensure I allot the appropriate amount of time for each lesson so pace your selves accordingly."

You can use a business scenario to explain that if their boss asks them to complete an assignment and they could not finish it at work by the end of the day, then they must complete it at home before they return to work the following day so the boss can take it into the important meeting he or she may have to attend.

Tip: While the students are responsible for budgeting their time appropriately during class, it is essential that you correctly estimate the length of time required to complete a task.

I have found that seemingly insignificant tasks can take up much more time than anticipated and accounting for that time is important to not rush or overwhelm students with an impossible deadline. Finding ways to eliminate or greatly reduce the impact of these non-learning tasks is helpful for getting the most out of class time while also reducing the amount of downtime (or time for students to get bored and misbehave).

For instance, logging onto the computer always takes more time than expected. Given that technology is imperfect, factoring in time for the computers to start up and time to troubleshoot any problems is important to staying on track while not eating into the student's time to complete assignments. My students know that before they do anything else, they must log into their computers so they may complete other activities more quickly.

A Typical Morning in My Classroom

As my students are entering the classroom, I give them a hi-five. I greet them with a smile and verbally welcome them.

Here is an example of how I address my students in the morning:

Boss: "Happy Monday! It's the first day of class and as far as seating arrangements go, you may sit wherever you want as long as you are not sitting beside someone who is hindering your performance in any way. If you feel you are sitting next to someone that may be disruptive to your performance, you must notify me discreetly and I will move your seat accordingly."

I explain they may remain at those particular seats unless there are behavior issues that warrant them being moved. I try and give them choices so they learn to be held accountable for their actions and behaviors.

If there are some performance issues that arise due to students disrupting others, I tell the Assistant Managers that I need to have a brief meeting with them after class (more about this role soon). I ask them what they thought about the current performance in the class. I discuss the importance of everyone needing to work efficiently so we can obtain all our goals and assignments asked from the boss.

I discuss how I would like the Assistant Managers to create a seating chart. I provide them a copy of a blank classroom layout and a list of student names so they can analyze and decide which seating arrangement would best suit the group. I give the Assistant Managers the ability to assess and make the necessary decisions so they learn to critically think what would make decisions best suited for the production of the team.

Once the assistant managers generate the seating chart for the class, I review it with them, make suggestions and/or revisions, and then the seating chart will be approved for the next class. At that time, the assistant managers will verbally communicate to their peers where their new seats will be as they are walking in the door. Students should not question the Assistant Managers as to why they are making that decisions; they need to understand there are constant changes and they need to adapt to them. They know they should not question the decision simply because they know they would not make decisions if it wasn't best for the team.

Particularly in the beginning of the semester, I work individually before, during, or after class so they find the right way to communicate announcements to the class. It is important for the students to develop a certain level of comfort with commanding the attention of the room, especially of their peers. Here is an example of what I might suggest an Assistant Manager say in this situation:

Assistant Managers: "We are your Assistant Managers and we have an announcement. We have a new seating chart because we need to ensure we are working in the most effective way as a team. We will walk around to each seat and verbally state who will be sitting at the seat going forward. So can everyone please step to the side and listen to our instructions so we can show everyone their new seat assignments."

Tip: It's amazing how the Assistant Managers learn how performance expectations impact production in the classroom and learn to act accordingly. By allowing them a role in implementing the classroom expectations, they gain the confidence and ability to lead others and set a positive example for their peers. In some cases, they will inform me of issues that may be occurring and I converse with them on their opinion as far as a solution so it immediately provides feedback.

Putting Expectations into Practice

In my classroom, every day begins roughly the same way for consistency purposes. Upon entering the classroom, students gather their materials and begin the warm up that is written with clear instructions on the Smart Board. I ask my students to put all of their Warm Up materials in the same document for every class.

For the Warm Ups, I provide some kind of prompt to get them thinking about either material we will be covering in this class or to review/ recite a topic that was learned from a previous class. I allow the students to use the internet to find inspiration for their responses, but I emphasize they need to always place the information in their own words. Oftentimes, I ask my students to research the definition of a particular business terms and explain the importance of not plagiarizing the information they find because it is someone's own ideas so it is against the law to do that. I then discuss what intellectual property means and how it's affects a person. This is a perfect time to discuss internet safety.

Boss: "So you truly understand the importance and the extent of what intellectual property means, it is the property of someone's own creativity. It's against the law to use it without permission or giving direct credit to the person. People could get fined or arrested if they plagiarize using someone else's work. You just need to remember that if you create it, you own the rights of the material."

During the first week of class, I remind students of their responsibilities when they come into class; however, after a few days, the students fulfill their responsibilities right away by immediately working on the Warm Up. I have had many people who visit my classroom that comment on how my students can practically run the classroom themselves because they are so organized and ready to work right when they come into class.

I will always provide a specific time frame to complete the Warm Ups so they understand that they must walk in and immediately begin working get right to work so they can complete their assignment on time. Usually I will say 5 minutes, 10 minutes or 15 minutes depending upon the subject. This specific time is listed on the Warm Up as well.

Why do I do this? Well, when you are employed by a business and you walk in in the morning, you don't usually sit at your desk and wait for someone to tell you what to do. It is your responsibility to find work to do or to begin tasks that were incomplete from the previous day. I want my students to understand how they can be self-sufficient and feel responsible for getting their work done. This is why I feel we need to prepare are children for career-ready futures—it is simply so they can understand that their performance will be similar to the way they will be working in a business environment.

While implementing Warm Ups will force students to practice many of your classroom expectations, they should also serve as a daily test for their soft and hard skills.

A good Warm Up should test their knowledge of a specific topic in relation to what has been taught or what will be taught, but it should also review their technical knowledge of the computer. As the students are completing their Warm Up, I will consistently walk around the room reviewing and commenting on their work.

I have provided some examples of Warm Ups that I use in my own classroom for 6th, 7th, and 8th graders to get you started. I put the Warm Up on the Smart Board so they can see the exercise right when they walk into the classroom.

6th Grade

What are three leadership traits that you possess? List in numbered format, black text, and highlight the three leadership traits in yellow. You have 10 minutes to complete this task.

Provide five reasons as to why being resourceful is important. Times New Roman text, 15 text, underline text, and list in square bullet format. You have 15 minutes to complete this task.

7th Grade

What are the 12 characteristics of an entrepreneur that we learned about yesterday? List in arrow bullet format, Arial text, 14 size text and blue font. You have 10 minutes to complete this task.

What are three types of businesses and what do they mean? List in numbered format, Calibri font, and size 16 font. Italicize, underline, and make all font green. You have 8 minutes to complete this task.

8th Grade

What is a résumé and why is it used? Provide a definition and explanation in your own words that are placed in 16 size text, italicize, and bolded. You have 8 minutes to complete this task.

What are the top five careers in our industry today? List them in a triangle bullet format, size 18 text, green text, and bold. You have 10 minutes to complete this task.

(Below is a particular warm up that is completed for all grade levels on the last day of class.)

Provide a one page Word document on what you learned in this Business Technology class and how it will assist you in the future. Use size 14 text, .3 margins, orange font, and bold text. You have 20 minutes to complete this task. You may utilize your organizational binder as a reference.

Now, remember the time is chosen based on the grade level so be cautious of making sure the time is sufficient based on the warm up question.

Boss: "Ok, everyone, time is up and we need to discuss and review the Warm Up. Who can tell me…"

Part II: Classroom Procedures

It is a well-known fact that all teachers need to demonstrate strong classroom management skills in order for optimal learning to occur. While in most traditional classrooms the teacher is the primary (and often only) mechanism for classroom management, I have created a classroom management system that is largely student centered.

My classroom operates as much like a real business office as possible. My students and I have roles and responsibilities to fulfill covering everything from time management to quality assurance. (I will describe the specifics of these roles in more detail in Part III.) Depending on the size of your class as well as other factors of your curriculum, you may determine that you need more or fewer positions than the ones I have in my own class. For example, first grade could use manager of the week instead of student of the week. It will provide a great way to explain to the students that their moms and dads work and they have to report to their managers, helping them feel important.

While this method takes time and practice to work smoothly, you will find that the benefits it brings to your classroom far outweigh the extra effort required to implement it. Effective classroom performance will include (but isn't limited to) better student communication, organization, and performance. When they understand that there is a process in place, they learn to adhere to it. (Besides, you will be getting a head start by reading this book that shares what works well in my classroom.)

There are numerous roles for which the students are responsible, including:

- Assistant Managers.

- Project Managers.
- Quality Assurance Managers.
- Marketing Managers.
- Scribe Managers.
- Transition Managers.
- Attendance Managers.
- Timekeepers.

All students have the opportunity to occupy one of the numerous leadership roles. The classroom is run like a business and operates seamlessly when individuals know their roles as well as their responsibilities as part of the team. It's amazing to witness students conforming to standard business practices because of how realistically the classroom models a real business.

It is important to remember that you also have a role and responsibilities as the "Boss". Just as I described in the Good and Bad Bosses portion of this manual, you must care that you are setting a good example in your own role and that you take the role seriously. Even if you are initially uncomfortable with playing the "boss" role, you will find that if you don't consistently act like the classroom is your business, you students won't buy into their roles either. The system relies on everyone taking part.

Classroom Performance

My ability to manage my classroom effectively and connect with the students as well as exceed in their performance is a measure of my true success. Knowing they are more prepared for the business world and are able to understand the importance of performance enables me to feel calm knowing they will be successful in anything they choose to do.

I primarily use this first manual in the series of four to discuss my management in the classroom and how my best demonstrated practices will prove ultimate results for every student.

Classroom role playing is a great way to bring the business curriculum to life and have the students participate by acting out different scenarios. You will find that much of my classroom structure is based on building a business environment into the day-to-day activities of the classroom. In this way, it becomes more natural to "act out" different scenarios.

Classroom Assessment

Assessment in the business world typically comes in the form of written performance appraisals and annual performance reviews. While it isn't enough in a learning environment to provide an assessment once a year, I still like to model the idea of performance appraisals in the classroom.

One of the most overlooked aspects of assessment is what occurs outside of official tests and quizzes. It comes in day-to-day critique and interaction with the students, which is truly considered formative assessments. This is something that happens on a daily basis in the business world, and it should happen every day in the classroom, too. The district in which I work stresses formative and summative assessments, crucial for the all students and needs to be practiced consistently.

Let's say you assigned a project for your students; they are in the middle of working and one of them has a question. If it was an office setting, the employee would go to the manager's office to ask questions, work out the problems, and design possible solutions. During this interaction, the boss might provide feedback on the status of the project; here, you in the role of boss would do the same on the work the student has completed thus far. The same goes with modifying students' role performance.

If you share any concerns, suggestions, or changes from the Assistant Manager, the students need to understand not to take constructive criticism personally and to understand it is for the betterment of the business. While this information isn't going on the student's annual review per se, it does provide him or her with informal helpful feedback about areas of weakness and improvements he or she could make. This prepares students for interacting in their future careers effectively.

Your students should be getting constant feedback and guidance from you formatively, which is why I seem to never be sitting down. I am always "live-reviewing" my students' work and providing them with constructive critiques. It's amazing how well the students learn to accept possible ideas being changed and complete the work asked by their "boss" and teacher.

Classroom assessments occur consistently during every lesson and don't necessarily have to be administered via a written test. I do provide pre-tests to gain an understanding of their knowledge of the subject and provide a post-test for retention of material at the end of the semester. In relation to information and assessments, I always remembered my teachers adding information to tests that they never even taught us and I found that very frustrating and stressful. "How do I know what I don't know?" All questions on my tests are covered in class so there are no surprises or added stress for the students when taking a test. I feel all tests should be administered fairly in order to diminish the anxiety that students feel about tests.

While the frequency and length of each test should be based on your own curriculum needs and district standards, it is very important to remember to work informal assessments into your classroom, especially when you are working with a classroom model with which the students are unfamiliar.

Classroom Transitioning

Our school has "QUIET" hallways, so it is rare that students are loud; if it does happen, the teachers and administrators remind the students of the expectations.

Tip: Transitioning is important and the students are very well aware of walking into the classroom and getting right to work because I explain that time is money in the business world. They need to work immediately as they arrive since they are being "paid" and the business is spending money on them to work there.

I prevent chaos in my classroom by explaining to my students that transitioning from one place to another is critical in the business world, especially if there are customers on the telephone line.

I often find that because of my classroom setup and expectations that the students enter the classroom quickly and begin working.

Boss: "I need all of you to come to the front of the room for a meeting and please remember that customers are on the line."

Most of the students will be loud the first time as they move their chairs, but I remind them that customers will not be able to hear the representatives providing advice on the telephones. If we provide poor service and cannot be bothered to provide a quiet environment, then they will likely cancel their purchases from the company and not buy any more products because of our unprofessional behavior. No purchases means no money coming into the company and its needs as well as wants need to be met.

Boss: "Please remember: It's about respecting the customer and their wants and needs. Always remembering you have a job because of the customer. Displaying professionalism at all times is crucial when dealing with customers. The customer is always right. Customers generate money for the company and you have your job because of the customer."

Since the students will make a lot of noise as they are moving their chairs to the front of the room for the first time, have the students return to their seats and sit down again. Now, verbally state again that customers are on the telephone line and they must be quiet while bringing their chairs to the front of the room for a meeting. Students begin to be patient and wait for others to move their chairs so it is completely quiet. They truly understand the impact of transitioning and being quiet in a business environment.

Students will learn that their collective contribution to the noise level affects the entire team and it helps them learn to work together to accomplish the tasks and understand how to respect customers.

The added benefit of this exercise is that transitions will occur more smoothly and less time will be spent in transition, which means more time for tasks and other activities will be accomplished.

Tip: Ensure students bring writing materials to "meetings" once you decide in which area within your room is most conducive for meetings based on the layout. If you are delegating tasks, they should not rely on memory to recall all of the details so they must write it down. By taking notes and being detail-oriented, it plays an integral part in performing successfully. Also, you can discuss the importance of cursive writing and how it assists them in writing faster in order to jot down the tasks the boss is listing off while still being able to actively listen to the directions.

Classroom Procedures

All teachers have their own procedures for their classroom and I have found that the more information that is communicated about what is expected to students ensures that they understand the overall rules for the class. Here is a sample of what I insert in the syllabus so they understand the importance of classroom procedures. (You can find the full list on my www.crteaching.com website and by looking at an example of a syllabus.)

Classroom Procedures
• Students must enter the classroom quietly and transition into the room by beginning to work immediately. Students will obtain points for smooth transitions on a weekly basis.
• Students must get to class on time. Tardiness will not be accepted unless you have a pass.
• Smile as you enter and greet your teacher. Once you have arrived, please sit in your seat, take out your organizational binder, and complete the "Warm Up" activity that will be posted on the smart board.

- Students must be prepared for every class. It distracts from learning time if the manager has to locate a pencil or paper. If a student forgets their materials, they should ask another student, so the class can begin promptly.
- Students must raise their hand and wait to answer.
- Students need to respect their teacher and classmates at all times.

Boss: "As your boss, I fully expect these rules to be followed *at all times*. If you fail to follow these rules, you will be called into my office and be disciplined according to the rules of the company (i.e. Student Handbook). Our office is a classroom, and it should be a safe environment, while ensuring performance and learning as our top priority. Also, in the real world there are always consequences so I want to make sure you truly understand what is expected once you enter into a working environment."

Student Organization

Organization is crucial for success in the business world. Imagine having to explain to your boss that you were late to a meeting (again) because you couldn't find the right report documents on your computer. Not only would that not be a very good excuse, it would also impact the way your boss would view you as a professional.

I try to instill in my students a sense of responsibility for the organization of their work. All students must have a binder with specific tabs that are what is covered throughout the semester that they put their work into and that I periodically grade throughout the semester.

Shorter-term organization: Explain how you as the manager must walk into a last minute management meeting with a specific worksheet that is in their organizational binder and see how quickly they can access it. The students learn to place specific documents in the labeled tabs so they know they can find it very quickly if their manager asks. It also reaffirms the importance of making sure they are organized at all times. They need to understand that when the boss asks something of an employee, they must quickly retrieve it and submit it as requested.

Longer-term organization: I provide due dates for various assignments and tell them that I am going to a meeting in the morning so they must obtain the listening worksheet located in the Actively Listening section of their binder. I explain that they need to have it on my desk for me at 8:00 am. Walk into class the next day and see who is able to provide the information to you.

Stressing the importance of being organized and knowing where documents are when their manager asks is critical. There will be many exercises where this is practiced throughout the semester, so the students learn to listen and respond quickly to their manager's requests. In the beginning of the class, you can see the students looking around at their peers and thinking, "oh no, this is going to be difficult." By mid-semester, all students are on task, completing assignments, and demonstrating great organizational skills. This skill is huge as far as standing out in the business world. In my classroom, I have an oversized dry erase calendar on the wall where I display all due dates for students to see. Rather than placing the due dates on the board myself, I will ask the Assistant Managers to write assignments and dates on the calendar during class.

Boss: "I recently got called into a meeting and management is requesting documentation from me. It's the leadership project worksheet that we completed a month ago, so please go to your binder and provide me with the information. I need to leave within three minutes, so please place precedence on this request."

Students: The students will quickly get their organizational binder and go to the worksheet that is specific to their manager's request and quickly hand it to their boss. All organizational binders have specific tabs so they know exactly where to access the information.

Explain to the students that it shows they have great organizational skills and their manager can always depend on them if they need anything. If not, there are consequences such as not getting assigned projects, receiving a lower rating on their performance appraisal regarding un-organization, not receiving a promotion, not receiving an increase in pay, and being placed on a performance plan. In addition, the manager themselves can experience the consequences from their supervisors as well if they do not hand in what upper management is asking for at the time.

Course Syllabus

I have found that syllabi are somewhat uncommon in the grades that I teach. However, I find that providing a written document with all the information that students need to know about my expectations and the course is helpful for giving them assistance in their own learning. If you need inspiration for your syllabus you can find a copy on my website at www.crteaching.com.

I find that it is important to stress the importance of the syllabus, especially if the students have not been exposed to this kind of document previously. You can place this as a Warm Up for students to research the purpose or you can verbalize it as the example states below.

Boss: "Who can tell me about a syllabus?" Have the students go to the internet and search for the definition if they have a computer accessible. If not, have them look it up in the dictionary. Remember to give the students a time limit for the task.

Verbalize and discuss each page of your syllabus. Have the students take turns reading the pages so the entire class understands what is requested of them for the semester. I ask that the syllabus be signed by the student and parent to confirm they are aware of all the expectations for the class. I also require that it must be returned to class on the specific date (usually by the end of the first week of school) as another example of deliverables and organizational management.

Boss: "Since I will be in your presence every day, I want your parents and/or guardians to understand my qualifications and the expectations for this class."

Tip: All classrooms are different as far as how you grade so you may want to decide to give points or a grade for turning it in. That way the students will realize the importance of the document.

Part III: Positions for Classroom Jobs

In this section, I have outlined the responsibilities of each position that I employ in my classroom. I wrote each position in a similar style to a job description that you might find posted on a company's website, so that each one feels like a real business position when the students review them.

Again, it is important for you to hold students to the responsibilities of their position. They need to feel like your classroom is an actual business and that you treat it as such.

Some positions are more intensive than others, so in certain descriptions I have added examples of what a student in that position might say as part of their job in the class. It is important for you to review the responsibilities of these positions with the students.

I use the classroom job positions model and it has been working effectively for years to parallel to the real world rolls. The chart at the end of this section provides examples of positions that currently exist within in the elementary classrooms and the jobs are parallel to the business world, but on a smaller scale. Why not have specific job responsibilities instituted into your classroom to bring career-ready awareness at an early age?

Selecting Positions

I allow the class to decide who gets the positions. I believe it is important for the students to know that they are responsible for the final decision, which makes them part of the team and helps them to understand that the decisions are fair. I firmly state that this is not a popularity competition and based on the description that I give for each job; they need to understand their personal qualities to help them be most effective in a certain role. They need to consider who specifically is going to make a positive impact on the team.

I begin by verbally providing the job descriptions for each position one by one and ask the students to raise their hand if interested. They then walk to the back (or front) of the room to stand in a straight line not facing the rest of the class so they don't see who is voting for them. Not only does this encourage students who might be shy to try for a position, it prevents hurt feelings and swayed voting if maybe a student's best friend did not vote for them (or if no one voted for them). I want this to be a positive experience and not have students be upset because they were not chosen.

I usually place my hand above the top of each student's head so the class can raise their hands and vote without the candidates seeing. I usually choose three "staff" for each job so we normally vote for the first person with the most votes and then once again in the same manner for the second and third person.

Once the students are chosen, I shake each one's hand and congratulate them all. To the students that didn't get chosen, I explain how important they are to the business. I convey that I am impressed that they showed an interest in the job and were there for me when I asked for assistance. I tell them to look me in the eyes and I make sure I communicate that I will never forget them being there for me as their boss. I never want any of the students to feel badly just because they were not chosen. I always allow my students to apply for as many positions as they would like, but they will eventually be assigned a role. I love seeing my students get excited about taking on more responsibility in the classroom.

Tip: If there is a student that tried to apply for a lot of the jobs and did not get chosen, then I reward them by making them my personal assistant so they feel a part of the team and boosts their confidence. It is important to recognize classroom dynamics in who gets selected for these positions, so sometimes it is necessary to step in and create special opportunities. This person simply would assist me in the beginning of class, writing things on the Smart Board, handing out supplies, asking if there is anything that I need completed such as hole-punching papers, organizing the room, or cleaning the dry erase board. There are so many other tasks that they can accomplish, but you can choose what is best for your classroom.

The Boss/ Business Manager/ Teacher

Qualities Required

- Oversees as well as supervises the business performance of students (employees)
- Focuses on the goals and accomplishments of the curriculum
- Observes, educates, and evaluates Education classes

- Ensures the students (employees) are meeting and exceeding all the goals and objectives
- Develops and implements strategies and lesson plans to improve learning
- Ensures students (employees) have the resources to complete all assignments
- Creates and leads hands-on activities for students (employees)
- Motivates students (employees) through incentives and positive interactions
- Provides constructive feedback in order for student employees to improve their work
- Possesses a professional demeanor
- Demonstrates strong verbal and written skills
- Demonstrates strong organization skills
- Demonstrates strong time management skills
- Demonstrates analytical and problem solving skills
- Assesses student employee learning styles
- Demonstrates quality in all aspects of work
- Continually makes efforts to provide a positive team environment

Boss: To introduce yourself as the boss, say, "My name is (say your name) and as your teacher, at this time I am now your _manager and boss,_ and you are my _employees_. I want all of you to understand that I am your boss and you must listen to directives that are verbalized AT ALL TIMES. Directives are specific instructions given by your manager that are essential for employee success."

What is an employee? An employee is a person who applies for a job and is hired at a company or business.

What is an employer? An employer is the company or business that hires employees to work for them.

Responsibilities

Motivate Employees

I always try to tell my students that I am happy that they are in my class and that I look forward to making a difference in their lives. I also tell them that my goal is to make sure they are succeeding and that they deserve a great education. I always announce and recognize when students are performing well. Doing this shows that I am excited about their work and it motivates the students to perform even better.

Enforce Active Listening

I explain to the class that they must listen to their boss at all times to ensure the business will run effectively and efficiently. They all know to stop what they are doing once I mention that I have a directive for the class. I provide a lot of multiple directives so I can see how well they listen. I communicate that I will always actively listen to what they have to say and I am requesting the same of them when I speak. I want them to know they are important and I will always listen to them.

Reward Employees

I reward my students by verbal praise and consistently tell them they are working well as a team. After monitoring their performance and if they meet their goals and complete their assignments early, I allow them to play typing games on the computer. A simple internet search will give your students plenty of options for typing games from which to choose. If they choose their own typing game, it will be more engaging and they will perform at a higher level.

Communicate Effectively

I always have team meetings in the front of the room (or a place that has a lot of space) where students bring paper and pencil to take notes. I instruct them that no matter what meeting they attend, a writing utensil and paper is mandatory. Some students use laptops or tablets, and those are acceptable, too, though it may take more work on your part to make sure they are focused on the lesson rather than playing games. They learn to take notes and understand that they need to remember information that their boss is telling them before they go back to work at their seat.

Instill Fairness

I explain if the boss is not fair, it will create an unhealthy environment as well as conflict within the classroom or office. Being fair creates student loyalty and a positive work environment. When I choose specific people, I take the attendance sheet and close my eyes and choose a student to complete the project. That way they know it is completed fairly. If you are tech minded, you can use randomized programs online to select a student's name, too, so students see more technology at work. I want to make sure that they know that they are all equal in my eyes.

Delegate

I delegate tasks and assignments to all the students within the classroom. This demonstrates confidence in the employee's abilities. Students enjoy experiencing and participating in special projects. It makes them feel important and encourages them wanting to learn as well as participate as a team member.

Focus on Teamwork

I consistently focus on team collaboration and stress the importance of the students always working together to accomplish the goals and assignments asked by their manager. It's amazing how they learn to assist others and communicate positively with their peers. I talk to them about thinking of the end result in order to work until the job is completed.

Provide Effective Feedback

I explain to the students how constructive feedback is important in the workplace and they should not take it personally if their manager has to revise or correct them on their performance. It's a way of learning from their mistakes and by applying the suggestions they will become stronger in their position.

In addition, I provide an example from my own work experience of having to create a presentation for a senior vice-chairman and working on it for 19 hours. The next day I walked in and he mentioned that the information had changed and I must re-do the PowerPoint for the meeting that afternoon. I smiled and told him that I would be glad to complete what is needed even though I was frustrated knowing all the time I spent on it. It's important to not show how upset I was and I wanted him to know he could count on me regardless of the changes. You always need to handle change in a positive and professional manner.

Assistant Manager Positions
Qualities Required

- Devotes one semester to the position

- Possesses a professional demeanor
- Demonstrates strong people skills
- Initiates self-motivation
- Evaluates students (employees)
- Greets visitors that arrive in the business classroom
- Answers telephone calls, "Business Technology, how may I help you?"
- Provides assistance to all visitors
- Handles stress and manages multiple priorities
- Demonstrates strong organization skills
- Demonstrates effective time management
- Accepts delegation given from the boss
- Assists in providing feedback to improve performance
- Creates classroom seating charts
- Acts as a mentor to other students
- Analyzes and solves problems when challenging situations arise
- Assists student employees on the computer
- Contributes to team effort by accomplishing related leadership skills
- Distributes student corrected paper assignments
- Analyzes class performance for increased production opportunities

Boss: "I need individuals that possess the following traits: Assertive, follows directives, focused, gets along with others, displays strong leadership skills, positive, performs at a high pace, likes to multi-task, effective communicator, problem solver, honest, decision maker, loyal, and fair."

Responsibilities

Once the Assistant Managers are chosen, challenge them by saying,

Boss: "Ok, Assistant Managers, I need you, please."

See how quickly the Assistant Managers get up from their chairs to show their understanding of urgency for the request. Most students that have not had this role (or not talked to others who have had the class) take their time at first and walk slowly to me. Raise your voice by saying,

Boss: "WOW, is that the way you want your manager to know you are ready and have the initiative to want to work hard for them? Remember TIME is MONEY so every minute counts in a business environment. Urgency is important in the business world so that we can accomplish all the necessary tasks and assignments to generate a high production to get the job done. The more work that is accomplished, the more money will be generated and our jobs will be stable."

All of the students usually chuckle. Have them sit back down and explain the importance that time is money and when any manager is requesting assistance, they must immediately stand from their chair and briskly walk to their manager. Make them realize that managers usually have very important tasks and directives, so they must quickly respond to the request; they must focus on the task at hand. Then, before the class is over, have the

Assistant Managers try their response again to approach the manager and make sure they quickly attend to the directive of their manager. If you have to complete it two or three times, then do so, but it normally only takes two times for them to understand their role as an Assistant Manager.

These "staffers" are also responsible for welcoming anyone that comes into the classroom and approach visitors out of respect. Assistant Managers should quickly go to the door as they hear it open and approach the individuals and shake hands while saying,

Assistant Manager: "Hi, my name is (student one) and I am one of the Assistant Managers. We are currently working on (project name) and if there is anything you need, please let me know."

It is required for Assistant Managers to introduce themselves. It's usually the ones that are closest to the door. Then the Assistant Managers walk back to their seats and begin working on the class assignment that their boss gave them.

The students need to understand the importance of approaching people respectfully and communicating professionally. You will see the students become respectful and understanding simply through practice and gaining the experience. Respect is one of the most important factors in everyday life when communicating with people and the students quickly realize how it is especially essential in the business environment.

Since I will be teaching and interacting with the class, my Assistant Managers are responsible for answering the classroom telephone as well; again, the ones closest to the phone will answer it.

Assistant Manager: "Hello, Business Technology, how may I help you?"

Assistant Managers need to communicate by taking turns as to which Assistant Manager will answer the telephone. It assists the students in gaining confidence to answer the telephone professionally and respond accordingly to the person on the other end. They must utilize their analytical and problem solving skills to address the situation since I will be teaching. The Assistant Managers will determine whether it is a situation where they need to interrupt me or they simply resolve the request by themselves (in most cases, they resolve it by themselves). It's usually the office requesting another student, so the assistant managers will go directly to that person and whisper in their ear quietly since class is in session.

Also, if you feel there is a decrease in performance from a student or you feel that student is not meeting the expectations for the course, then assign them as an additional Assistant Manager to give them a positive initiative to model. That means you may have four assistant managers. Explain that you need an additional assistant manager and how important they are to their team to meet and exceed goals and expectations, while producing over and beyond what is being asked. Explain why you chose him/her because of their potential and ability to communicate effectively. Make sure you choose a strength that is evident in their performance. Mention the specific strength and ability he/she possesses so they begin to feel confident and want to learn. It's amazing how a student all of a sudden improves their performance because there is a higher expectation. Each student that has had the experience of becoming an Additional Manager stresses the importance of how being a part of the team makes them want to perform at a higher level. I have had 100% success in utilizing this strategy.

Tip: I emphasize positive reinforcement and provide guidance and support on a daily basis.

Tip: A meeting with the other Assistant Managers needs to take place so they are notified that there was an addition to their team. It's proven that consistent communication plays a role in creating a positive environment for all student employees. From my experience in the business world, reviewing employee feedback, effectively communicating with the employees through team meetings, email, written and one-on-ones, was very important to everyone in the company.

Project Manager Positions

Qualities Required

- Ability to devote one semester to the position
- Possesses a professional demeanor
- Demonstrates strong people skills
- Displays effective team building skills
- Initiates self-motivation
- Evaluates students' wants and needs
- Possesses excellent communication skills
- Demonstrates the ability to handle managing multiple priorities
- Demonstrates strong organization skills
- Demonstrates effective time management
- Accepts delegation given from the boss

- Acts as a mentor to other students (employees)
- Analyzes and problem solves when challenging situation arise
- Responsible for tweet text creation and messaging daily
- Assists students (employees) on the computer
- Contributes to a teamwork atmosphere through related leadership skills

Responsibilities

Project Managers are responsible for managing any team project throughout the semester as well as coaching, supervising, process improvement, self-development, and planning. There are various class projects assigned throughout all of my Career Education volumes.

For example, you may have the Project Managers assist in organizing the selection of job positions in the beginning of the semester. They may go to the front of the room and begin conversing with their team to select specific students for classroom jobs, using the same voting process as was used for their "role" selection.

Also, the boss may assign a class project that needs to be completed within a certain time and the Project Managers handle the job, working cohesively with the team to achieve quality results. Below are some of the announcements the project manager may say.

Project Manager: "Our boss just assigned a project and we need to complete it in 45 minutes. Let's have a meeting to decide the steps to accomplish the project. Who can provide some ideas where we want to start with this?"

Project Manager: "We have only five more minutes to complete the project before our Quality Assurance Managers check our work so what is the status right now as far as completion?"

Quality Assurance Manager Positions

Qualities Required

- Ability to devote one semester to the position
- Possess a professional demeanor
- Initiates self-motivation
- Evaluates students' (employees') wants and needs
- Possesses excellent communication skills
- Demonstrates the ability to handle managing multiple priorities
- Demonstrates strong organization skills
- Demonstrates effective time management
- Accepts delegation given from the boss
- Acts as a mentor to other students (employee)
- Analyzes and problem solves when challenging situations arise
- Responsible for tweet message clarity and accuracy
- Contributes to team effort by accomplishing related leadership skills
- Prepares quality documentation and reports
- Validates quality processes

- Enhances organization reputation
- Maintains and improves classroom performance

Responsibilities

Quality Assurance Managers are responsible for preventing mistakes or avoiding performance problems. When assigned various projects throughout the semester, the Quality Assurance Manager must exude confidence and ensure quality requirements are being fulfilled. The boss will be the person responsible to assign the specific projects and the Quality Assurance Managers must converse with the project managers and then re-check the project that is completed before distributing the results to management.

Quality Assurance Manager: "I know you just recently completed a project and I would like to check the quality of the team's work."

Quality Assurance Manager: "Let's take a look at what you have completed and talk through your reasoning so we can figure out whether this is accurate or not."

Marketing Manager Positions

Qualities Required

- Devotes one semester to the position
- Receives approval from parents and/or guardians to open a class social networking site (where we place project updates, reports for parents to read, and more)
- Possesses a professional demeanor

- Demonstrates strong people skills
- Displays effective team building skills
- Initiates self-motivation
- Demonstrates the ability to handle managing multiple priorities
- Contributes to the team effort
- Manages the classroom social networking site, including messaging topics
- Distributes rewards to the students (employees) participating in the social networking initiative
- Develops marketing strategies to increase followers
- Monitors and reports daily status of the marketing strategies utilized
- Ensures accessibility of an electronic device to take pictures and post on a daily basis.
- Tweets on the classroom's social media on a daily basis

Responsibilities

Blended learning is extremely important in the classroom and these managers are responsible for marketing the classroom's social networking site throughout the semester. They need to communicate to the class the number of followers before the beginning of each class and discuss ways to improve the production of social networking for the social site. Blended learning is an integral part of learning and the students thrive on it.

For example, as soon as the Marketing Managers arrive to class, they ask the boss who the students were that tweeted. They must ask me simply because all tweets will come through my personal feed and once I retweet their comments, all students that are in the social network will see each student's remarks about the class.

Once the boss verifies with the Marketing Managers that particular students tweeted, the students will receive a reward distributed by the Marketing Managers. The reward can be as simple as a piece of gum.

Now, I know there are students that may not be allowed to have a social networking account, so they may ask other students that do have an account to tweet for them. This can be another "role" in the classroom - Social Marketing Analyst - in order to follow home rules and work with classroom tasks. That way, those students will still receive a prize for making an effort to increase the awareness for the initiative. (Note: The students are not allowed to take out their phones unless authorized by me.) Here are some examples of what Marketing Managers will do.

Marketing Managers: "We are your Marketing Managers and we have an announcement. Currently, we have ____ followers and we would like to recognize the students that tweeted. Who tweeted from last class?"

Marketing Managers: "We would like to take some pictures of you working on our class assignment, so please continue working as our boss has requested."

Marketing Managers: "We will now take a video of the class working on the project."

Transition Manager Positions

Qualities Required

- Devotes one semester to the position
- Possesses a professional demeanor
- Demonstrates ability to organize
- Assesses and provides support for the boss and students (employees)
- Observes students (employees) as they enter the business classroom
- Records and assesses student's (employee's) performance transitioning to their seat as they walk in for the day
- Verbalizes absences to the boss
- Verbalizes students (employees) that did not transition effectively to the boss

The Transition Managers will stand by the door with a clipboard and a copy of the class list to document points for students that walk in and begin producing. It's basically taking attendance and observing students that are transitioning effectively and getting right to work.

Responsibilities

The Transition Managers should be the first person to arrive in class and obtain the clipboard with the class list from my desk. (See transitioning chart on the next page.) In my class, I give free points for transitioning to my standards. These free points build throughout the semester (max of 10 per week) and it assists in increasing their grade because of their performance behavior as well as toward prizes such as pizza parties. It is the responsibility of the Transition Manager to remind students of this. The Transition Manager will allot two points for each student on a daily basis for simply walking in the classroom and following instructions on the warm up that is placed on the Smart Board.

It's basically teaching the students to begin producing as business expects since they are being "paid". If they talk while walking and/or sitting at their seat, then no points are recorded for that day. The purpose of this ongoing exercise is to emphasize to the students that in a regular work environment, managers want them to begin producing as soon as you walk into work. So at the end of the week students could receive a total of 10 FREE points if they abide by the rules of transitioning effectively—free points is their pay!

Tip: Please remember to communicate to the students that you, as their boss, are always present and seeing exactly who is not transitioning effectively. That way, you can validate any documentation of points not given from the transition manager, if for some reason a student did not get points for a particular day.

Tip: If a student does not obtain points for the day, there should never be a disagreement from the students to the Transition Manager since they understand what is expected of them and know why they would not receive points. ***Please take note you should also be present during this time.***

Transition Chart Example

(T is the note for talking and it takes off two points for each "T" per day)

NAME	MON 2-Sep	TUE 3-Sep	WED 4-Sep	THU 5-Sep	FRI 6-Sep	TOTAL
Arthur	T		T			6
Regina						10
Isabella						10
Lena		T				8

Attendance Manager Positions

Qualities Required

- Devotes one semester to the position
- Possesses a professional demeanor
- Demonstrates ability to organize and assess quality of work
- Observes students (employees) present in the classroom
- Records and assesses student (employee) attendance
- Verbalizes absences to the boss

After the Transition Managers have completed recording the transition points as well as attendance, they will provide the Attendance Managers with the clipboard. Upon checking for accuracy from the Transition Managers as far as student's attendance, the Attendance Managers tell the boss who is absent; they must sign into the computer so they may record attendance. Once attendance is recorded, they go back to their seats and the Boss double checks their work.

Emphasis is placed on accuracy and quality of work. If there is an input error, the Attendance Managers notify the Transition Managers immediately if there was a mistake and to be more cognizant of student (employee) attendance.

Responsibilities

The Attendance Managers must understand that they need to retrieve the clipboard from the Transitions Managers if they forget to give it to them. It is a huge responsibility to ensure attendance gets recorded correctly into the system for the day—this is just like database integrity and management, a large role at many companies. They must always approach the boss no matter how busy the lesson may seem and ensure their job is completed for the day. In the event a student walks into class and is tardy, the Attendance Managers need to ensure they speak with the boss in order to adjust the attendance in the computer. This provides the students with accountability and ensuring they are completing their job thoroughly.

Attendance Managers: "Excuse me, Boss. Susan Collins and Kirsten Sooy are absent for the day."

Boss: "Thank you."

Scribe Manager Positions

Qualities Required

- Devotes one semester to the position
- Possesses a professional demeanor
- Demonstrates strong writing skills
- Initiates self-motivation
- Ability to handle a fast paced business environment
- Ability to manage multiple priorities
- Demonstrate strong organization skills
- Demonstrate effective time management
- Demonstrate strong written and communication skills

Responsibilities

The Scribe Managers verbally summarizes in the beginning of class what was learned in the previous class and what the students will be learning in the present class.

The Scribe Managers will take notes in a notebook of their choice after every class on what was learned throughout the lesson and then the following day they approach their boss and ask them what will be taught in the class for the day. They will then verbally summarize to the class what was covered in the previous class and what will be covered for that day. They always have to ask their boss in the beginning of class (in a small meeting) what is going to be covered for the day so they can communicate the specific information to the class. See below for a scenario that would take place before the lesson starts as the Scribe Manager speaks to the class.

Scribe Manager: "Excuse me, Boss, can you please inform me as to what will be discussed in class today?"

Boss: "Sure, we will be researching the definitions of the characteristics utilizing the internet and talking about the three types of businesses."

Scribe Manager: "We are your Scribe Managers and we have an announcement. *(First manager can say this).* Yesterday, we covered entrepreneur characteristics. *(Second manager can say this).* And today we will be researching the definitions of the characteristics, and utilizing the internet."*(Third manager can say this.)* Please come to the front of the room for a team meeting."

Students/Employees: As the Scribe Managers indicate that there is an announcement, all students (employees) immediately stop what they are doing and listen to the Scribe Managers' announcement. Their body positions should be facing the Scribe Managers and actively listening at all times. This shows respect and their initiative to listen at all times and will become aware of the objective for the lesson.

Timekeeper Positions

Qualities Required

- Ability to devote one semester to the position
- Possess a professional demeanor
- Demonstrates strong communication skills
- Initiates self-motivation
- Demonstrates effective time management

Responsibilities

While the basic duties of a Timekeeper are apparent in the job title—tracking the time throughout class—there are plenty of tasks and challenges to the daily routine, from working on projects or to the everyday work that is expected in class.

Boss: "Time and production is crucial in the business world and you must pace yourselves accordingly to accomplish tasks and assignments asked by your boss, so that is why we need a time keeper."

At first, remind the Timekeeper on occasion about verbally mentioning the time to the class just in case they may have forgotten. They may feel a little awkward at first, but continue to assist in reminding them so they begin to feel confident in their performance as the timekeeper.

The Timekeepers are responsible for monitoring the time throughout the class. See below for responsibilities.

- Verbally raises his or her voice out loud and says, "Five minutes until class is over," informing students of the specific time throughout the class so students are aware of managing their time effectively and can pace themselves accordingly during various assignments.
- It informs the teacher the amount of time that is left in the class to ensure all material is covered for that particular lesson.
- Projects his or her voice, so everyone can hear the time being called throughout the class period. A lot of times it all depends upon the assignment and how many times the timekeeper may announce the time. See below for an example:

Timekeeper: "30 minutes."

Timekeeper: "15 minutes."

Timekeeper: "5 minutes."

Timekeeper: "1 minute."

The Timekeeper should not have to get the boss' authorization to verbalize the time spoken out loud during class. Usually it is when the teacher has stopped talking. They know they should not interrupt the teacher.

Positions for Classroom Jobs Chart

I always generate and post a classroom jobs chart to provide a team awareness of who is responsible for each specific classroom job. If there is ever a question as to who is responsible, the students can reference the worksheet that they create in one of the assignments to replicate this chart, which they place in their organizational binder. It emphasizes how they all need to work together as a team to accomplish the goals and objectives for the company.

This is a perfect way to add accountability to the team and enhances the ability to effectively manage a classroom for ultimate results.

Then, after the staffers were chosen, I ask the Project Managers to ensure the students are aware of who is responsible for each position by verbally asking them to recite the names out loud to the class. It's amazing how students will remember and begin to assist one another if they cannot recall. Again, it's the students learning to work together as a team to accomplish a common goal.

Always leave blank lines in the job chart as you may find other roles to fill, too. If you have more than 24 students in your class, add the remainder students to a Marketing Manager's project group. This group can use more people if need be so they can focus on Twitter to promote more interaction. You can also add other business positions to the mix.

Getting Started with Lesson Plans

Now that you have an idea as to how to manage the classroom effectively with the information that I have provided, attached are four detailed lesson plans that I use starting week one (our first day is the selection of positions). They can guide you on the specific structure of each lesson and how the student jobs are integrated throughout the class. These lesson plans are typically for the first week of class.

Day One: Follow the information mentioned in the previous chapter for implementation of the syllabus and job positions.

Day Two: Welcome and ice breaker is to get to know the students and focus on presentations and communication skills.

Day Three: Goals lesson is to assist in learning to set goals for future career success.

Day Four: Learning styles lesson provides the opportunity for each student to learn about their specific learning styles in order to study and learn more effectively.

Day Five: Creating Microsoft Word graphs with the learning style data from the previous lesson.

Other lesson plans will follow in additional volumes in the other manuals; those manual topics will include Careers, Entrepreneurship, and business soft skills.

These additional manuals will provide career-ready curriculums. The business foundations taught will instill life-long lessons for any child. My goal is to assist you in providing the best business management practices to unveil successful and career-ready students.

It's never too early to start preparing our students for their futures. As you can see, career-ready positions are easily adaptable to any classroom, will prepare students to understand the expectations, and expose them to the requirements of the world in which they will be working in someday.

Please remember that you do not have to utilize all jobs within this book, so you can decide what would best suit your classroom and integrate accordingly. If you want to use all of them, then that is great as well. Understand it does take time to institute the implementation with continuous reinforcement, so please be patient.

In discussing the career-ready expectations with the students, you can relate to a social studies module about careers and how their particular jobs exists in the real world. Tell them how important their jobs are so they understand it's crucial in order for a company to run effectively. Please don't think that the words of the career-ready job positions are too complex for the younger grades because when it becomes a normal expectation throughout each day, you would be surprised how the students retain it as they are "living" it. Communicate that their parents are working in the business environment and it will promote great family discussions about the similarities regarding school and work.

Career-Ready Job Positions for Elementary School

CURRENT K-5 STUDENT JOB POSITIONS	PURPOSE OF STUDENT JOB RESPONSIBILITY	JOB POSITION OPTIONS FOR ELEMENTARY STUDENTS
Mascot of the Week	Basically each student is recognized on a weekly basis so the entire class gets to know them as a person by providing pictures, biography and shares several items that are special to them.	Assistant Managers
Line Leader	This student is responsible for being the leader in the front of the line and setting an example for all the other students to exhibit excellent behavior.	Assistant Managers
Messenger	This student writes down on a piece of paper of the absent students for the day and communicates missed assignments upon their return.	Scribe Managers
Paper Monitor	This student is responsible for passing out graded papers and worksheets.	Assistant Managers
Pencil Sharpener	This student is responsible for sharpening student pencils for the day.	Project Managers
Door Holder	This student is responsible for holding all doors in which the class has to enter or exit.	Transition Managers

Table Washer	This student is responsible for washing tables within the classroom and cafeteria.	Assistant Managers or Project Managers
Classroom Lights	This student is responsible for turning out the lights as the class leaves the classroom.	Quality Assurance Managers
Book Monitor	This student is responsible for returning student books to the library and cleaning the classroom bookshelf.	Marketing Managers
Name Pins for Attendance	Each student is responsible for taking a clothes pin and placing it in the basket to let the teacher know if they are present for the day.	Attendance Managers
Mailbox Monitor	This student is responsible for making sure all handouts are placed in the student's mailboxes.	Quality Assurance Managers
Calendar Changer	This student is responsible for placing the new date on the calendar every day.	Scribe Managers
Unified Arts/Specials Chart Organizer	This student is responsible for changing the unified/special chart so all students are aware of what special they are supposed to attend for that day.	Project Managers
Chair Monitor	This student is responsible for taking down the chairs of the students that are absent for the day.	Project Managers

Floor Monitor	This student is responsible for checking the floor to ensure there are no items misplaced on the floor.	Quality Assurance Managers
Crates/Lunches	This student is responsible for taking the lunches down to the cafeteria for lunch.	Project Managers
Calling Tables	This student is responsible for observing tables that are quiet.	Quality Assurance Managers
Homework Helper	This student is responsible for ensuring all students receive the necessary homework at the end of the day.	Quality Assurance Managers
Timer	This student is responsible for turning on a timer for classes throughout the day.	Timekeeper
Board Eraser	This student is responsible for erasing the dry erase board.	Project Manager
Helper	This student is responsible for making sure the classroom pets are fed and the cages or aquariums are cleaned.	Assistant Managers

Part IV: Enacting Your Lesson Plans

Remember, these are my classroom lesson plans that I use for 6th, 7th, and 8th grade that we complete the first week of receiving "roles" and the first day is the selection of those positions for students (employees). You will see some redundancy for job positions, but I want you to understand where they would normally fit in a lesson plan. There are templates for you to modify as you see fit. For example, if you use Apple products, you will need to adjust the Word to Pages, Excel to Numbers, and PowerPoint to Keynote. These are to help you see how they work in my classes and to help you build a business-centered learning environment in your school. Also, not every day uses all the various sub-headings for exercises—don't be concerned something is missing if all types of classroom "sessions" are not on each day.

Example Day Ice Breaker

Students will learn about one another through an ice breaker while focusing on proper presentation and communication skills.

Students Entering the Classroom

As the students are walking into the classroom, stand by the door and say:

> **Boss:** "Good Morning and Happy Tuesday."

This plays a huge role in showing the students that you are happy to see them and it provides a warm welcome into the classroom. I consistently demonstrate this on a daily basis and the students come to expect it ow. They actually say it to me first a lot of times.

Tip: The Transition Managers should be the first students to arrive to class and retrieve the attendance clip board. They will begin taking the attendance and recording FREE transition points. Once the Transition Managers have completed their assignment, they must give the clipboard to the Attendance Managers.

Tip: Once the Attendance Managers receive the clipboard from the Transition Managers, these students re-check the attendance for accuracy. They go to the boss (which is me) and ask to sign in so the attendance can be recorded. They tell the boss the names of the students who are absent and the boss records it in the computer system.

Tip: As students are entering the classroom, the Scribe Managers immediately go to the boss and ask what is going to be covered for the day. They jot it in a notebook and make an announcement to the class. All students should have direct eye contact and position their bodies toward the Scribe Managers that are making the announcement.

Scribe Managers: "We are your Scribe Managers and we have an announcement."
- The first Scribe Manager may say, "During the last class, we worked on assigning job positions."

- The next Scribe Manager may say, "In this class, we will be working on getting to know one another through an ice breaker."

- The third Scribe Manager may say, "After our warm-up we have a team meeting so please come to the front of the room."

- After the meeting, they immediately all return to their desks to begin working on the class Warm Up.

Tip: Marketing Managers will always follow the Scribe Managers. They will make an announcement on how many Twitter followers are on our (my personal) Twitter account. They will ask the class who tweeted and they distribute gum or lollipop as a reward. Marketing Managers can take turns distributing the reward.

Then they may say:

Marketing Managers: "We are your Marketing Managers and we have an announcement. We have 366 followers; who tweeted after last class?"

Tip: Assistant Managers will also always pass out graded papers after the Marketing Managers make their announcement and they complete their Warm Up.

Warm Up

Have the students enter the classroom and read the below information that is listed on the Smart Board. Have them log onto their computers, with specific instructions for a drill.

- Log onto Microsoft Word
- Click FILE then NEW
- Click FILE/SAVE and name your document WARMUPS
- Type your name in the upper left hand corner in black/Arial/12 font
- Type the subject BUSINESS TECHNOLOGY in the same size, color, and font right below your name.

Complete the following information:

PERSON – *Choose a favorite person that you admire*

PERSONALITY TRAIT – *Choose a personality trait that you appreciate about that person*

PASSENGER CAR – *Choose the type of car that you would you would drive in with your favorite person*

PLACE – *Choose your favorite food that you would like to eat at a restaurant with your favorite person*

If the students do not have access to a computer, they may list it on paper.

Boss: "You have 10 minutes to complete this task." *(*Make sure you always provide a time for completion of tasks and assignments since the real world requires it.)

Timekeeper: "Six minutes left for the Warm Up." "Two minutes." And so on.

The Timekeeper will specify how much time is left for the Warm Up so the students can pace themselves accordingly in order to complete the assignment.

Introduction

Boss: "Hi, my name is Mrs. Foxwell and I'm so excited that you are all in my class. You are going to experience a great semester with interactive learning and it will prepare you for a career-ready future. So going forward, I am your boss and you are my employees. Before we start, we need to establish some questions to ensure you understand what is going to being covered in class today:"

1. Why is it important to get to know your peers?

2. What are some mannerisms you need to remember when you are speaking to people?

3. What is constructive feedback and why is it important?

Boss: "Now, let's start by having each student stand and verbalize what their 4 Ps. We will start on one side of the room and follow rows. I would like each student to stand in front of the class and state their 4 Ps."

- **PERSON**
- **PERSONALITY TRAIT**
- **PASSENGER CAR**
- **PLACE**

Tip: This is a great way to get to know the students and they also learn about what other classmate's interests are as well. Explain the importance of working together to achieve goals needed for a business and getting along with one another as a team.

As the students begin communicating their 4 Ps, interject at times and ask questions such as:

- PERSON: Why that particular person? What's his or her occupation? How did he or she inspire you? Why is he or she so important to you?
- PERSONALITY TRAIT: Why is that trait important to you? Do you have the same trait? Give me an example of when that personality trait made an impact on you.
- PASSENGER CAR: Why that particular type of car? What color is the outside of the car? What color is the interior of the car?
- PLACE: Why that particular restaurant? What specific kind of food? Do you like booths or tables?

Communication Development

Boss: "Before you begin speaking and telling the class your 4 Ps, it is crucial to remember:

- To be respectful and actively listen at all times.
- Provide eye contact with the person speaking and never have your back toward the people to whom you are speaking. So if you are standing and students are sitting behind you, you must move the position of your body to ensure your back is not facing anyone. It's out of respect to the person or to people with whom you are talking.

- Project your voice at all times when speaking to an audience. Pretend you are in an auditorium and most of the audience is sitting in the back row. Would the speaker be able to project their voice enough for all of us to hear? **YES.** Otherwise, if the audience could not hear the speaker, the people listening wouldn't want to pay attention to the presentation. You spent a lot of preparation for a presentation, so making sure the audience is engaged by speaking loudly is important. Trust me, I've been in plenty of presentations where it was difficult to hear the speaker so I tuned out what was being presented.

- Keep your hands crossed or behind your back so physical distractions don't occur, such as moving your hands, twirling hair, moving your arms, etc. Also, verbal distractions such as "Like" or "Um" should be avoided during a speech or verbal communication. Even adults say um and like all the time and it's very frustrating. So, my goal is to try and ensure you become cognizant of not saying it while presenting or speaking to others."

Boss: "It's always so much fun to get to know everyone, so I will go first. The person who I admire is Michael Jordan because even though he is a very famous NBA basketball player, he is a strong business person as well. I played basketball at the same time he did so I've always had an interest in his overall performance. The passenger car that I would use to drive him is a black Saleen Mustang. Cars have always been a passion of mine, and that type of car is my favorite type. The place I would take Michael Jordan to eat would be a seafood restaurant because I love seafood. The personality trait that I admire about him is being humble. He's had great success and always remained humble. Ok, who wants to go next?"

Tip: Many times it's much easier to start on one side of the room and work your way around to the students so they know when they need to speak next. This way it also saves on time and not having to ask who wants to go next.

Tip: The Timekeeper should be announcing the time throughout the class. Depending upon the assignment, the Timekeeper may randomly choose times to announce before the end of class. They know they must be respectful and wait until there is a time where I'm not speaking and they verbally announce the time. They may say longer or shorter times, such as 30 minutes or 5 minutes. At first you will need to prompt the Timekeeper by likely saying, "Timekeeper?" Usually, they quickly look at the time to announce it. You may have to continue reminding them the first week or so. Once they get used to it, they become consistent and you will never have to worry about the amount of time left in class.

Student Independent Development

Each student will stand and verbally discuss what their 4Ps are to the class. This will take approximately 40-50 minutes while interjecting and asking questions. It promotes conversation and it releases a little bit of stress. The students feel more comfortable speaking in front of others. This is a skill they will use for the rest of their lives so experiencing it at a young age is crucial in order to stand out in their future careers.

Providing Constructive Feedback

Be consistent in providing professional feedback to the students as they state their four Ps to ensure they understand all the criteria in speaking effectively in front of an audience. Make it a fun atmosphere and ensure all constructive criticism is positive and interactive. Even though I have to correct students at times on their physical distractions, the students are very receptive of how hard it is to remember all the ways to speak in front of an audience.

Developing students' presentation skills and providing feedback becomes fun for all the students and a lesson they will remember for the rest of their lives. It's amazing how some of the more quiet students really immerse in the activity since it is interactive. I explain to the students that there is a really high percentage of people who are frightened to speak in front of others, so it's normal to feel nervous. It takes practice so the more they practice, the better they will become.

The students begin to recognize their own mistakes (such as saying "um" or "like" as well as physical distractions). It's incredible how they correct themselves and restart their sentence knowing it should be communicated the correct way. It's always funny to hear students tell me how they attended a presentation and the speaker said "um" thirty six times. They begin to realize the proper way of speaking and demonstrate it on a daily basis.

Boss: "Wow, it's so exciting hearing about your four Ps and it's nice knowing a little bit more about you on a personal standpoint. I look forward to a fantastic, yet productive semester with all of you. You are all important to me and I sincerely want you to walk the path of success and become prepared for a career-ready future."

Closure

Tell the students what a great job they did and explain how nice it was getting to know all of them. Revisit the questions that were asked in the beginning of the lesson.

1. Why is it important to get to know your peers?

2. What are some communication skills that you need to remember when you are speaking to people?

3. What is constructive feedback and why is it important?

Boss: "Now I would like you to turn to your neighbor and discuss what you learned about three of your peers today."

Walk around the room as the students are discussing what they learned and observe them. Give the students at least three minutes to speak to their peers.

Students Departing the Classroom

Boss: "Great job today, see you on Wednesday and we will be learning about your specific types of learning styles."

Boss: "Great job today, Sam. I liked how you displayed strong communication skills during your presentation."

Boss: "Mandy, it was nice how you assisted your peer with the Warm Up."

Boss: "Cole, it was so wonderful to hear about your four Ps and your interest in cars."

Example Day Setting Goals

Students will learn about goal setting and how it's important for their future success.

Students Entering the Classroom

Boss: "Good Morning and Happy Wednesday."

As in the first example, the five roles complete the following "start of class" assignments:

Transition Managers take the attendance worksheet on the clipboard and begin recording FREE transition points.

Attendance Managers re-check the attendance and provide the boss with absences.

Scribe Managers ask the boss what is going to be covered in class.

Marketing Managers make an announcement on the amount of Twitter followers and distribute rewards.

Assistant Managers return graded work.

Introduction

Boss: "We will be discussing goals today so before we start, we need to establish some questions to ensure you understand what is being covered in class today:

1. Why do we need to write goals?
2. What are academic orientation goals?

3. What are goal orientation objectives?
4. What are personal goals?"

Development

Boss: "Now, let's talk about goal setting and why it's so important. What do you think an academic goal means? ***It's something that you worked towards in school or work to achieve.*** Let's talk about things to remember when we write goals."

Tip: Remember to list or verbalize the below goals and stress the importance of them having:

- Measurable goals so you can track your progress as you go.
- Inspirational goals that give you a reason to invest the time and effort into achieving them.
- Concrete goals that define exactly what you want to accomplish.
- Realistic goals that work with your personality and lifestyle.
- Obtainable goals so that you don't become discouraged.
- Micro goals move you closer to your vision one step at a time.

Tip: The following are the types of questions I make sure are covered in the discussions, letting the students set the pace of discussion:

ACADEMIC ORIENTATION

What questions can you ask yourself about achieving academic goals?

1. What are you trying to achieve?
2. What do you hope to accomplish in the next year?
3. What do you hope to accomplish in five years?

GOAL ORIENTATION

What reminders or steps will help you move toward your vision?

1. Don't procrastinate.
2. Focus on the end result.
3. Remain positive.
4. Learn from your mistakes.
5. Focus on a healthy life style.
6. Communicate effectively.

Tip: Verbally ask the students the questions and have them write their answers down on lined-paper.

Student Personal Goals

Boss: "My mother instilled a lot of goals for our family. I'm passing out a list of personal goals that she instituted on a daily basis. These goals made me the person that I am today. Place a checkmark next to the goals that you already possess and highlight the ones where you think that you need to improve."

Student Personal Goals

	Goals I currently achieve	Goals I want to improve
To look on the bright side of things		
To remember things happen for a reason		
To work extremely hard for goodness to follow		
To know it's ok to make mistakes, as long as you learn from them		
To treat people the way you would want to be treated		
To live for the moment		
To always work out your differences with others		
To wish the best for everyone		
To look at life as a journey and enjoy the ride		
To be thankful for all you have in your life		
To think positive		

To believe in yourself		
To be creative		
To understand others and the way they live		
To accept criticism		
To strive close towards perfection		
To never make excuses, be like NIKE and JUST DO IT		
To have a strong sense of purpose		
To never say the word "CAN'T"		
To take risks		
To be patient		
To make the most out of life everyday		
To take opportunities when it comes your way		
To dream big		
To not settle for second best		

To laugh and have fun		
To be honest		

Student Independent Development

Boss: "I want you to write your personal goals in cursive. I am distributing a cursive alphabet worksheet to assist you with cursive writing. You will need to use cursive or script for checks, to sign legal documents like your driver's license and even at the store when you use your debit or ATM card. So this is important practice."

Tip: Instruct the students that the lined paper and worksheet need to be placed in the right pocket of their organizational binder. This serves as a reminder of the goals that they set and continue to work on achieving them.

Closure

Boss: "You did a great job writing your goals and I'm hoping you will remember the significance for your future career. Now let's revisit the questions that we talked about in the beginning of class."

1. Why do we need to write goals?
2. What are academic orientation goals?
3. What are goal orientation objectives?

4. What are personal goals?

Boss: "I would like all students to please stand up and discuss with your peers what goals are the most important to you for your future."

Students Departing the Classroom

Boss: "Great job today; see you on Thursday and we will be learning about you own learning styles."

Example Day Learning Style Exercise

Students will learn about their own specific learning styles through a computer assessment. You can also obtain worksheet assessments as well.

Students Entering the Classroom

Boss: "Good Morning and Happy Thursday."

As in the first example, the five roles complete the following "start of class" assignments:

- **Transition Managers** take the attendance worksheet on the clipboard and begin recording FREE transition points.

- **Attendance Managers** re-check the attendance and provide the boss with absences.
- **Scribe Managers** ask the boss what is going to be covered in class.
- **Marketing Managers** make an announcement on the amount of Twitter followers and distribute rewards.
- **Assistant Managers** return graded work.

Warm Up

Have the students enter the classroom and read this information (listed on the Smart Board):

- Go to an internet search engine like Google and type ***Learning Style Assessments*** in the search bar. You can choose from a variety of computerized assessments that will determine their learning style.
- Create your Warm Up document and list your findings in Arial, 14 font and blue text.

Complete one of the assessments and analyze your results.

- You have 10 minutes to complete the assignment.

Introduction

Boss: "Before we start, let me ask you some questions and raise your hand if you agree:

1. How many of you read information in a book and can't remember what you just read?

2. How many of you sit in a class and can't remember what the teacher is saying?

3. How many of you complete assignments and don't understand the overall purpose of it?"

Tip: Discuss the importance of learning in the best possible way so they understand their own specific learning style. Explain how they can retain information; by reviewing their results, you as a teacher will understand how each student excels as they each pinpoint their own learning style.

Boss: "My job is to ensure we both understand the best way in which you learn. It will assist you with retaining material in the most effective way and I will be able to identify the best way to teach you to comprehend information."

Class Development

Boss: "We are going to review three categories of learning styles in which people learn. Please understand there is not one specific way to learn and that is why we all have to study differently." (*Note that you would post on the Smart Board to review each type with the class.*)

Tactile Learner

You learn via a hands-on style. You understand and remember things by physically doing it to remember. You prefer to touch, move, build, or draw what you learn; you tend to learn better when physical involvement occurs. You need to constantly be interactive in order for retention of material to take place.

As a tactile learner, you enjoy putting things together and physically working on specific learning strategies to understand the material being taught. Tactile learners tend to be coordinated and have good athletic ability. You easily remember things that were done, but may have difficulty remembering what you visually saw or heard in the process. You often communicate by hand gestures and touching, such as using a handshake or head nodding.

Tactile learners learn best this way:

- Trace words with a finger.
- Move while learning.
- Study for 30 minutes and then take a 15 minute break. Then complete the steps again.
- Participate in activities that involve touching, building, moving, or drawing.
- Complete hands-on activities and projects.
- Chew gum, walk around, or rock in a chair while reading or studying.
- Use flashcards to review or learn material.
- Sense of touch is beneficial while using a computer to process the information.

Always remember that you need to have hands-on learning, not just see things, in order to learn in the best possible way.

Visual Learner

You learn best by visually seeing things to process the information, like reading or seeing pictures. You can picture what you are learning in your head and you learn best by using methods that are primarily visual. You like to see what you are learning.

Visual learners often close their eyes to visualize or remember something. You may have difficulty with verbal directions and sounds may easily distract you. Color is exciting and you are attracted to bright colors. You also like information that is imaginary.

Visual learners learn better this way:

- Sit near the front of the classroom so you feel you are close and ready to learn.
- Having a yearly eye exam to ensure you are able to see correctly.
- Always utilize flashcards to learn information.
- Visualize information being taught.
- Make sure you hear information that is being read aloud.
- Write down the information being delivered.
- Draw pictures to help explain new information.
- Color coding information is helpful.
- Avoid all distractions during study times and have everything quiet.

Always remember that you need to **see** things, not just hear things, in order to learn in the best possible way.

Auditory Learner

You learn by hearing and listening to what is being said or taught. You understand and remember things that are being said. You understand information by the way it sounds and you have an easier time understanding verbal instructions. You have to read out loud because you have to hear or speak it to understand it.

Auditory learners learn better this way:

- Have someone ask test questions by reading out loud so you can hear it.
- Record yourself and then listen to the recording.
- Make sure you are sitting where you can hear what someone is saying.
- Study new material by reading it out loud to yourself.
- Use flashcards to remember information and read out loud to yourself.
- Always read assignments out loud before starting.

Always remember that you need to **hear** things, not just see things, in order to learn in the best possible way.

Tip: For example, you may choose to pre-write on the dry erase board the total breakout of your learning types in the class:

NAME	**Tactile %**	**Visual %**	**Auditory %**
Eva	**55%**	**25%**	**20%**

All learning styles will differ for each student. Have each student stand and individually tell the class what percentage was the highest for their type of learning style in their assessment. Then instruct each student to go to the dry erase board and write his or her name in cursive and add the specific percentages for each learning style.

As the students have completed verbalizing and writing their learning style plus percentages, go to the board and point to all the learning style percentages. Confirm for them that all students learn in distinct ways and it's important to focus on their specific learning style to excel in life. Everyone processes information differently.

Separate the tactile learners in a group, visual learners in a group, and auditory learners in a group. Have each group discuss ways in which they feel are most beneficial when studying or learning information.

Student Group Development

Boss: "Each type of learning style needs to move to sit together in a group. Designate someone to type a Microsoft Word document and in a number format list add the five ways your group learns best. Make sure all of your names are on the document. List the title as the strongest learning style in 18 point font and the remainder of the document should be in number format, Arial, black, and 14. Print your document. You have ten minutes to complete this exercise and then we will present your strategies to the class."

Tactile group may say:
1. Use flashcards to study.
2. Make sure you study in a quiet place.
3. Have another person read questions and then answer on paper.
4. Use computer activities to help.
5. Moving and learning assists in remembering information.

Visual group may say:
1. Always obtain a yearly eye exam to ensure you are able to see correctly.
2. Always utilize flashcards to learn information.
3. Try and close your eyes to visualize information being taught.
4. Make sure you hear information that is being read to you.
5. Always write down the information being delivered.
6. Draw pictures to help explain new information.
7. Color code information.

Auditory group may say:
1. Have someone ask you test questions by reading it out loud so you can hear it.
2. Record yourself and then listen to the recording.

3. Make sure wherever you are sitting you can hear what someone is saying.

4. Study new material by reading it out loud to yourself.

5. Use flashcards to remember information and read them out loud to yourself.

6. Always read assignments out loud to yourself before you start.

Tip: On the next page, you'll see a chart that I would share with the groups before every presentation, so they understand how they earn points. The chart helps them understand expectations.

Presentation Rubric

ORGANIZATION AND DEVELOPMENT	SCORE CRITERIA	SCORE RESULTS
In the introduction, the speakers introduced their group prior to the presentation.	1	
The speakers explained why the group was presenting.	1	
The speakers delivered the information requested by stating five ways to effectively learn with their specific learning style.	5	
The speakers had the document that was requested of them in the correct format. Make sure all names are on the document. List the title of the specific learning style in 18 font and the remainder of the document should be in number format, Arial, black, and 14.	6	
In the conclusion, the speakers thanked the audience for their courtesy in listening.	1	
In the conclusion, the speakers worked together cohesively and planned the presentation out effectively. They also asked if the audience had any questions.	2	

VERBAL AND PHYSICAL PRESENCE		
The speakers had good eye contact with the audience.	1	
The speakers used clear and distinct enunciation.	1	
The speakers seemed relaxed and poised.	1	
The speakers exhibited no distracting physical mannerisms.	1	
The speakers projected their voices for the audience to hear the presentation.	1	
The speakers seemed to be enthusiastic throughout the presentation.	1	
		22

Closure

Boss: "Why is understanding your learning style important for the success of your education? Speak to your peers and tell them two ways you will now be able to become more focused on learning effectively."

Tip: Monitor the students to ensure they are engaged in speaking with other students and walk around the room to listen to conversations.

Students Departing the Classroom

Boss: "Great job today; see you on Friday and we will be working on learning styles charts in Microsoft Office."

Example Day Learning Type Chart Exercise

Students will learn how to create Microsoft Office charts for their specific learning styles.

Students Entering the Classroom

Boss: "Good Morning and Happy Friday."

As in the first example, the five roles complete the following "start of class" assignments:

- **Transition Managers** take the attendance worksheet on the clipboard and begin recording FREE transition points.

- **Attendance Managers** re-check the attendance and provide the boss with absences.

- **Scribe Managers** ask the boss what is going to be covered in class.

- **Marketing Managers** make an announcement on the amount of Twitter followers and distribute rewards.
- **Assistant Managers** return graded work.

Warm Up

As the students walk into the classroom, have them read the below information that is listed on the Smart Board.

It may look like this:

- Please list all three learning styles and provide a brief definition for each one in Microsoft Word.

List in bullet format, Arial, 16 font and bold. All students should retrieve their individual daily Warm Up document and complete the exercise.

Introduction

Boss: "Before we start, we need to establish some questions to ensure you understand what is going to being covered in class today:

1. Why do you have to create charts?
2. What are the different types of charts?
3. How do you change the color and lines in a chart?
4. How do you add data percentages to a pie chart?"

Class Development

Boss: "I need all students to come to the front of the room to discuss how to create a chart in Microsoft word." Review the instructions on the Smart Board:

1. Click on the on the Microsoft Word icon.
2. Click File, new/blank document/file/save as/computer/documents/learning styles as the file name.
3. Write your name and date on the top right hand side of the document.
4. Click tab 3 or 4 times to get your cursor where you want to insert your chart.
5. Click insert/chart/pie chart.
6. There will be a data table that appears where they will have to insert their learning styles percentages.
7. As the data is input in Microsoft Excel, the pie chart should be changing with the data you are placing in the table for the Microsoft Word pie chart.
8. Right click, add data labels to add percentages or any other label options by right clicking on the chart.
9. Right click on the pie chart and in the upper right hand corner of your screen it should display, format text effects. Click on the paint can and add different colors to the pie chart and/or add different options for the text.
10. If time allows, you may also choose another chart to display the learning styles percentages.
11. Pass out a copy of the worksheet that restates what has been displayed on the Smart Board that explains how

to create a chart in Microsoft word and utilize as a reference.

Student Independent Development

Boss: "Now I need you to go back to your seats and begin creating various charts for your personal learning styles." (Charts may look like the ones below.)

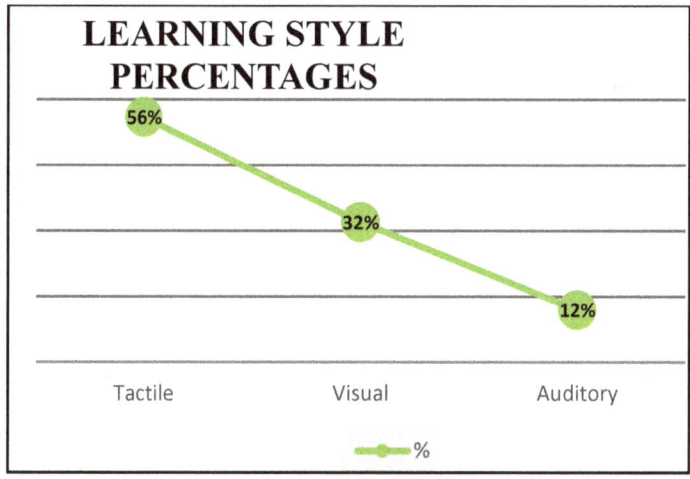

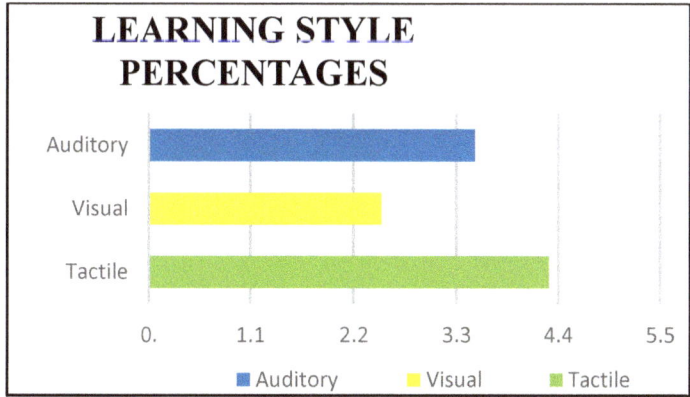

Boss: "Upon completing your charts, please ensure you get my approval to print. Upon approval, print the charts and place them in the front of your organizational binder. This will be a reminder of how you need to always think about your learning styles and the best possible way you learn."

Student Group Development

Boss: "I need to attend a meeting, so I want all of you to complete a project for me. I want to ensure you all work together as a group and pace yourselves accordingly because I will be back within 25 minutes. Please understand I have to take the results to my afternoon meeting so completing the project on time is very important.

"Where are my Project Managers and Quality Assurance Managers? You are responsible for making sure you gather three groups for each learning style by choosing the learning style percentage that was the highest. This project must be completed when I return, so good luck."

Tip: Go to the door and open it and shut it while staying inside your classroom, having them understand that you left for your meeting, then remaining to observe their performance. The students assigned leadership roles may progress the assignment in a similar manner as below.

Project Managers: "We are your Project Managers and we have an announcement. Our boss has instructed us to choose the highest percentage that you received from your learning styles yesterday and separate into groups. We have 14 peers in tactile, eight in visual and three in auditory. Our total number of team members is 25. So if you received your highest percentage learning style as a tactile learner, stand to our right. If you received your highest percentage learning style as a visual learner, stand to our left. And if you received your highest percentage learning style as an audio learner, stand directly in front of us.

"Now, take the number of team members in your group and divide by 25, which is the total amount of members on our team, to obtain the overall percentage of the specific learning styles. You may use your computer calculator or we have calculators. Once we have the total percentages of all three different learning styles, we need to create charts in Microsoft Word. We will list the percentages on the dry erase board." (Note: It may look l like **Tactile = 56% Visual = 32% Auditory = 12%.**)

"Please reference the instructions for creating a Microsoft Office graph that we received yesterday so you can use it as a reference. Please print once completed. Remember we only have 25 minutes. We will ensure our Timekeeper provides a status of the time so we can work accordingly." (Note Timekeepers will announce the countdown of time remaining.)

Quality Assurance Managers: "Ok, our project is complete, but let's double check the information to make sure we fulfilled all the criteria that our boss asked of us. Let's review what we accomplished. Please provide all the charts so we can review them."

After 25 minutes passes, **Boss:** "I'm back from my meeting and I hope everyone worked well together to accomplish the assignment that I asked of you. Project Managers and Quality Assurance Managers, please provide me with an update on the project."

Project Managers: "The entire team worked well together and completed the project efficiently as well as accurately.

Here are the copies from the project so you can take them to your meeting this afternoon."

Quality Assurance Managers: "We double checked the work and the project is 100% accurate."

Boss: "Thank you for completing the project on time so I can and provide the results in my afternoon meeting."

Closure

Boss: "Let's review the questions that we talked about in the beginning of class and see what you know about them now:

1. Why do you have to create charts?

2. How do you change the color and lines in a chart?

3. How do you add data percentages to a pie chart?

"Speak to your peers and ask how teachers could implement different learning strategies so you learn more effectively."

Tip: Monitor the students to ensure they are engaged in speaking with other students by walking around the room to listen to the conversations. Focus on the student's ideas so you can possibly incorporate them into your curriculum.

Students Departing the Classroom

Boss: "Great job today. Now go have a great weekend, everyone, and I will see you next week!"

A Note About Lesson Plan Consistency

As you can see, all the lesson plans are consistent and students adapt very well to career-ready instruction. Providing hands-on activities, blended learning and live scenarios strengthens the student's interest where they want to learn more. They become very receptive to the overall class expectations and convert to opportunities for higher level of learning.

Applying these strategies is proven to work and enables students to build a stronger foundation for their future.

About the Author

After living in Delaware most of her life and graduating from Bloomsburg University of Pennsylvania with a degree in Elementary Education, Eva Foxwell obtained a job in Silver Springs, Maryland, as a first grade teacher where she was a natural educator. However, listening to parental advice, she left teaching to enter the financial services world with two promotions within three months during the summer.

The decision to work in banking yielded more income as well as changed her life forever in a very positive way. Within two years, she was promoted two more times, when a Senior Executive Vice President became her mentor. Honing to her expertise and experience with education-based projects, she became an education manager, who in turn educated the corporation on a new computer system.

Continuing to move up on the education track, she became a Senior Education Manager making a positive difference for the people within the company. After 14 years, three children, and increasing family responsibilities, she replied that her time with the company was coming to a close. She assisted her husband with his business; with a turn of events, she went to work for the insurance company that had to cover fire damage to the repair shop that they owned.

Routinely identified for her education background and her entrepreneurial skills, Eva helped this newest business open three more offices in five years and gained more knowledge about another service industry.

Eva's husband and her own hard work ethic focuses on the needs of the customer. She brings this passion to her classroom, where she was recognized by the vice principal of her younger children's school. Starting just a few days a week substituting, it has turned into a daily vibrant educator role where she now shares the "tricks of the trade" with other teachers around America and continues the special events such as the Networking Event and The Stepping Toward the Future to ensure her students are prepared for what's to come.

In 2015, Eva was a Delaware Superstars Education winner and a Teen Ink Magazine Educator of the Year as a result of her methods for creating successful programs.

She encourages all teachers to connect with a local business, ask for an informational interview, and a tour for students. Integrate what the local businesses need with the exercises accomplished in class. Highlight the skills the employer finds are most important for individual success in their business and translate that to the classroom.

You can purchase Eva's other curriculum guides on her website at CRTeaching.com: Teaching Business Soft Skills, Teaching Entrepreneurship, and Teaching Career Exploration.

Follow her on Twitter @Eva Foxwell to observe all the activities and assignments that her students are currently posting as a 'live' peek into her classroom.

Also, if you would like to be added to a private Facebook group for teachers currently utilizing the Managing The Classroom strategy, request Eva Zanolini Foxwell on Facebook and she will add you to the group. This group provides shared tips, questions, reference materials, and strategies to effectively implement the Managing the Classroom curriculum.

www.ingramcontent.com/pod-product-compliance
Lightning Source LLC
Chambersburg PA
CBHW040329300426
44113CB00020B/2695